Jiu-Jitsu – The Basics

Christian Braun

Jiu-Jitsu – The Basics

Meyer & Meyer Sport

British Library Cataloguing in Publication Data
A catalogue record for this book is available from the British Library

Jiu-Jitsu – The Basics
Christian Braun
Maidenhead: Meyer & Meyer Sport (UK) Ltd., 2006
ISBN: 978-1-84126-171-3

© 2006 by Meyer & Meyer Sport (UK) Ltd.
2nd Edition 2009
Aachen, Adelaide, Auckland, Budapest, Cape Town, Graz, Indianapolis,
Maidenhead, New York, Olten (CH), Singapore, Toronto
Member of the World
Sport Publishers' Association (WSPA)
www.w-s-p-a.org
Printed by: B.O.S.S Druck und Medien GmbH
ISBN: 978-1-84126-171-3
E-Mail: verlag@m-m-sports.com
www.m-m-sports.com

INDEX

Foreword by the Author

Even when I was a small boy, the subject of Martial Arts always fascinated me. However, my father, whose work colleague was a successful Judoka, forbade me to learn any of the Martial Arts, because he had misgivings about my health due to the number of injuries he saw in his colleague. And so it came to pass that, as a youth, I learned dancing for about 6 years and had begun the run-up end phase of training for tournaments. But this all was soon brought to a halt as my dance partner gave up the sport of dancing and I didn't feel too much at home in the environment of tournament dancing. Parallel to this I played for about two years in the school basketball team – a sport that I regularly include in my warm-up training still today. However, we play practically with no rules – there's simply a basketball, two baskets and lots and lots of players. I dropped onto this way of playing from Thomas Cruse, the ex-vice president of Progressive Fighting Systems in a seminar in 1996 in Munich. He emphasized the many advantages of this training as well as the way it optimizes one's agility.

When my dance partner at the time dropped out of dance training, I was just 17 years old and was looking for a new challenge. It was clear that I wanted to take up Martial Arts training – but which one? So night after night, I visited clubs and schools that had Martial Arts on the program and I looked at the various styles.

I noted that in Judo the main emphasis was on throwing the opponent and ground-fighting. To do this you must be able to grip the opponent first of all. But what does the Judoka do when the attacker comes forward with short rapid strikes and kicks so that grabbing him[1] is very difficult?

So I then looked at Karate training. Here I noted that the athletes were very good at distance fighting. Strikes and kicks can be well defended against and counter-attacks were carried out perfectly and dynamically. But what does the Karateka do when he is locked in an embrace? What does he do when he is on the floor and someone is sitting on him? What about defense techniques against handguns?

---

[1] Note: to avoid repetition and make easier reading, whenever the male form is used, the female form is also equally meant to be included.

I have also been to Aikido training and the tricks that the Master used, so that I didn't manage to bend his arm or even lift it, completely fascinated me. Today, I know that generally these are just tricks and I can learn them by myself. However, it wasn't only the tricks that gripped me but also the way in which throws are executed. Indeed it occurred to me that the partner generally carried out extremely wide, round and slow attacks. For example, in an attack by a trained boxer, I would have severe thoughts as to whether the Aikidoka would be able to block the punches or even be able to execute these round sweeping defensive actions. Also defense against kicks against the shins (low kicks), as they are executed in Muay Thai (Thai boxing), would be very difficult to maintain in Aikido in my opinion.

Despite all this, all these different styles are admirable and I can understand anyone who trains in one of these sports. My focus was, and still is, on self-defense and in my opinion, and as demonstrated above, the individual systems and styles are only usable with limitations. I could also not detect any effective defense against weapons in these systems. Although, in places, there was training for defense against weapons, it was in a form that I, personally, don't hold as realistic.

What is realistic will now be a question that one or other reader will ask. This question concerns particularly the type of weapon. I am absolutely sure that an unarmed defense against someone trained to use a knife can never end up without injuries being inflicted – even if one has trained for 20 years in the martial art. Therefore, for me, there are three golden rules for unarmed self-defense:

1.   *Get to hell out of it!*
2.   *Get to hell out of it! – and*
3.   *Get to hell out of it!*

Running away is not cowardly, it's actually rather clever. However, one doesn't always have the chance to be able to escape before being attacked. Therefore, it is sensible to learn techniques that will increase the probability of surviving such an attack. In my opinion, the best principle concerning defense against weapons is to use the Philippines' system/style (Arnis, Kali, Eskrima...). For ground-fighting, sports such as the Brazilian style of Jiu-Jitsu (e.g., from the Gracie or Machado families) or Luta-Livre are recommended. For fighting at a distance, Muay Thai (kick boxing) is recommended.

An optimum would be a mix of these sports. Twenty years ago I wasn't aware of this kind of detail. I was looking for a self-defense system that would give me a solution for all reach distances and against armed attacks, and this was Ju-Jutsu or Jiu-Jitsu.

Because of its full content, Jiu-Jitsu can only integrate a few of the techniques/ principles from other types of sport, otherwise the test program would be too large and it would not be possible to learn it. It is, therefore, wise to train in a number of other types of sport in order to specialize in various areas. For the weapons area, I take lessons with Jeff Espinous, the founder of the sport Kali-Sikaran and Technical Director of the IKAEF, as well as one of his students Timm Blashke. I have also learned from many others such as Bob Breen, Mike Inay, Emanuel Hart, Paul Vunak and Thomas Cruse inter alia. Jeff and Timm are, however, the instructors that have taught me regularly now for several years.

In the area of ground-fighting, it was in 1996 that I first came into contact with Thomas Cruse (1st Dan BJJ and then Vice-president PFS). In the old JJ test program there were only a few techniques for ground-fighting. Tom has a black belt in Brazilian Jiu-Jitsu and impressed me even then. Following this meeting I also looked for special courses here and in the meanwhile I have been able to train with several top trainers. Amongst these are Roy Harris (black belt in BJJ), August Wallen (Head Coach Shootfighting) and nowadays with Andreas Schmidt, the Head Coach of the European Luta-Livre Organization, where I am also an instructor.

I would like to thank my students Saskia Braun, Alexander Emmering, Swen Harz, Robert Zawis, Gabi Rogall-Zelt, Gunter Hatzenbühler as well as my friend, student and training partner Waldemar Wodarz who have all helped me with the photography for this book.

All that I have experienced in the last twenty years in my Martial Arts interest was only possible with the support of my wife Angelika, who has let me get on with my passion for the sport without a murmur.

Frankenthal, May 2005, Christian Braun

Foreword by the Technical Director of the German Ju-Jutsu Association (DJJV e.V.)

EXPERT KNOWLEDGE – PUT TOGETHER PERFECTLY

Ju-Jutsu – this is the art of modern self-defense.

In Ju-Jutsu, the techniques and concepts are linked together and developed from various martial arts in order to produce an effective system of self-defense as well as to create a good medium for fitness and leisure sport. Everyone can discover themselves and find a way to practice a sport and martial arts together.

In the last few years, this martial art has developed significantly and seen many changes. Elements from other martial arts styles (some unknown up till now), fresh knowledge about the science of movement and sports and changes in violent behavior in society have all made these changes necessary in order to keep pace with the use of a modern, flexible system. It is probably due to this and the variety contained in our system that experts have not yet managed to produce such a text-book. Thus it has taken almost four years until Christian Braun has managed to do so.

It is in Christian Braun's character that in his training and teachings he always works with meticulous perfection. I have never met any other Budo instructor, who has analyzed, structured and assessed the art of movement sequences in such detail as he has. This sort of perfection can found in this book. With a mass of examples and nearly a thousand illustrations, every Jiu-Jitsu and Ju-Jutsu athlete or follower can see how to execute all the possibilities, techniques and combinations exactly and use them in practice training.

As a result, this book represents an important step in progress for our martial art's fighting system and surely will be very soon a set text-book for every Jiu-Jitsuka/ Ju-Jutsuka.

Karlsruhe, February 20, 2005
Joachim Thumfart
Technical Director and Secretary (Youth Division) DJJV e.V.
Assistant Sports Director JJIF

WHAT ARE Jiu-Jitsu and Ju-Jutsu?

Jiu-Jitsu and *Ju-Jutsu* mean, roughly translated, winning by using the 'gentle art' of giving way. The root of this system is in the martial art Jiu-Jitsu, which was practiced by the Samurai as an unarmed method of self-defense. It consisted mainly of throws, joint-lock and Atemi techniques (punching and kicking techniques). Various people have taken individual groups of techniques out of the Jiu-Jitsu system and developed new types of martial arts such as Judo (Throwing). As a result the origin of many of the different types of martial arts can be traced back to Jiu-Jitsu.

For the most part, *Ju-Jutsu* emerged from the best technical elements of the Japanese sports of Judo, Karate and Aikido. The sport of Ju-Jutsu has benefited since its foundation by the integration of effective techniques from other martial arts. Where, earlier, it was more those techniques from the Japanese systems (Judo, Karate, Aikido etc.,), latterly in the last few years it has been influenced by the Philippine systems such as Kali, Arnis or Eskrima for fighting against weapons, and the Russian system (Sambo), the Brazilian system (Brazilian Jiu-Jitsu and Luta-Livre) for the areas of "change-over from standing to groundwork" and "ground-fighting techniques". The straight blast and the blocking foot kick, the sequence of defense actions in the three-step contact (Hubud) and the continuation of the Atemi technique (called **Trapping** in the respective jargon for the sport) came from Wing Tsun (with also other spellings), Jeet Kune Do and also Kali. The shinbone kick (low-kick) comes from Muay Thai and is also a very effective technique. Exercise forms have also been integrated from Boxing and Kick boxing.

Bruce Lee said once, "Absorb what is useful". Using this maxim, it would appear that Ju-Jutsu has really grown since its inauguration.

Jiu-Jitsu and Ju-Jutsu both cover fighting at all distances (within kicking, boxing, trapping, throwing and ground-fighting distances). They also permit one to close the gap to the opponent and give defense against armed attacks (pistol, stick and knife). Both, Ju-Jutsu and Jiu-Jitsu, have become very similar nowadays, as the effective techniques of Ju-Jutsu have often been included in Jiu-Jitsu as well.

If you are interested in Jiu-Jitsu training, you can contact me directly by sending an e-mail to:

Christian.Braun@open-mind-combat.com
www.open-mind-combat.com

Etiquette

Etiquette can be divided into four areas:

- Behavior in the Dojo
- Discipline
- Cleanliness
- Loyalty

After you have received the information about where and when Jiu-Jitsu or any other self-defense sport will take place, there comes the time when you first enter the training hall (called *dojo* from here on in) and come to terms with the etiquette required.

When entering the dojo, the trainee bows for the first time. This expresses that he accepts the rules of the dojo and comes to train with a "pure spirit".

The students and the Masters collect together in the dojo. It is generally sensible to lay down the training mat if throwing training or exercises where the partner is to be brought down onto the ground are being practiced. This should be carried out jointly by all those taking part in the training (students as well as Masters). Turning up late for training should be avoided. If it happens once, the person late must go quickly to his trainer, bow, apologize for his lateness and then take part in the training once his trainer allows him to carry on.

But let's go back a step or two. The mat has been preferably laid down on the ground with everyone joining in. The trainer now enters onto the mat first. As long as he is a black belt, he can be addressed as *Sensei* (Japanese for instructor or teacher). In some Japanese martial arts the term *Sensei* is used for the Grand Master (higher than 5th Dan). In others there are different terms used such as *Renshi*, *Kyoshi* or similar.

If emphasis on maintaining the etiquette in a dojo is uppermost, then the *Sensei* is never addressed using his first name. Also in such cases, one should be at least 1m away from the *Sensei* when one is talking to him.

First of all, of course, there is the bow. Should the *Sensei* give one of his students the honor of being his demonstration partner, that student immediately goes down on one knee as the *Sensei* announces this to the group. When the student realizes that the *Sensei* wants to carry out the demonstration, he stands up and bows and waits for instructions.

I tend not to be that traditional, and for me in my dojo everyone is addressed by their first names. This is something that each *Sensei* has to decide for himself within his dojo. However, whenever I go into another dojo, it is obvious that I will maintain the rules of that dojo.

After the *Sensei* has entered the mat, the other Masters and students follow on. As soon as both of your feet are on the mat you make a short bow. This shows that you are ready for the training and you will try to do your best. The same occurs when you leave the mat.

Before anything starts, the *Sensei* and the students and the Masters line up as follows: The *Sensei* stands in the middle of the mat. The students stand in front of him and the Masters stand to the left. These stand in order of belts. It has become generally normal that the black belts do not have to stand in the ordered line-up. This is because the Dan belts often don't have chevrons on the black belt to indicate their grade. For the students it's quite clear, however, as the first in the line are the brown belts, then the blue, green, orange and yellow, with the white belt at the end. At the beginning and end of each training session each time there is the greeting. This can be done either in a standing position or kneeling down. Because of time restrictions, if the *Sensei* uses the standing greeting, he gives the first graduate in the line-up a sign. This graduate then greets the *Sensei* saying "*Sensei* ni rei". The *Sensei*, as well as the students and the Masters hold their arms down to the sides of the body with the palms of their hands lying down the seams of the trousers. They now bring the left leg together with the right one and make a short bow. Now, training can begin. This ritual is slightly different from dojo to dojo.

More traditional, but also more elaborate is the greeting kneeling down – something which I personally like to have done, because I use the time it takes to concentrate on the upcoming training or to have a good feeling for the training just ended. The *Sensei* gives the command "Seisa." To be completely traditional, he should then turn slightly to the right and kneel down on the left knee. Turning to the side has historical roots. Earlier, the Samurai wore heavy armor. If they had simply gone down on one knee, they would have toppled over sideways. The left leg is used firstly because the Samurai wore their swords on the left side. Should the opponent, who is opposite draw his sword, then the defender was also able to do so. Following the left leg you then kneel down on the right leg. The toes are flat on the ground. The *Sensei* now sinks down onto his haunches as if he wanted to sit on his heels, but just as he reaches the end position he lifts himself up again slightly in order to lie his feet flat on the ground and he then sits down. The Masters and the students now do it in turn. In other Japanese sports, such as for example many Jiu-Jitsu organizations, the procedure of kneeling is done in turn from the highest graded participant down to the lowest.

The person kneeling at the front of the group now gives the command, "Mokuso!" Everyone closes the eyes and prepares themselves mentally for the training. Similarly when the end greeting is done, they let the past training session go briefly through their minds. After about a minute, the same person gives the command, "Mokuso jea mei – (short pause) – *Sensei* ni rei." The first part of this ends the concentration phase and the second is the greeting to the instructor.

GREETING IN THE KNEELING POSITION

Now the *Sensei*, Masters and students all make a bow. First of all, the left hand, held out forwards at about 45°, is placed on the mat. The left is used first so that the Samurai could still draw their swords with the right hand in an emergency. Then the right hand is placed down. When both of the flats of the hands (actually it's more the finger tips) are on the mat, there is a short, mutual bow. With the Samurai, they used to watch each other constantly so as not to give the other the opportunity to do a surprise attack. Now the right hand is brought up onto the thigh of the right leg (along the lines of the same reason above), and then the left hand on to the left thigh. The *Sensei* lifts his bottom slightly, places his toes back on the ground and lowers his bottom again, before he positions his right leg and foot

out to the right forward side. Then comes the left leg. As soon as the *Sensei* is standing up properly again, and not before, then the other Masters and students go through the ritual. In the standing position there is a short bow made where the participants pull the left leg into the right leg. Then the training can begin, or likewise the session is brought to an end.

Another type of bow is done when you go off with a partner to do, for example, a joint exercise. Here the bow reflects respect for one another and says to the partner, "Thank you for training with me", or vice versa, "Thank you for having trained with me."

 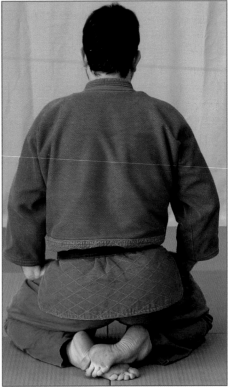

Position of the feet – Greeting in the kneeling position

The second big factor for me is 'discipline'.

The important thing for me here is that the students strive to be punctual or apologize correctly if they haven't made it on time for the beginning of training. Also the student shouldn't leave the training prematurely without having helped to put the mat away. A further point is attending training regularly. As a trainer, it's often difficult for me even to get to training punctually, but I make every possible effort to make sure that I'm not late. When only a few students are there and one of them says that he doesn't feel like participating, then I ask myself what has become of the etiquette. Things have changed in the last twenty years or so. Students or club members often treat the *Sensei* without any particular respect and see him as an easy entertainment pushover, whose training sessions are there to be used or not used, just as they like. Despite all the changes, there's not much new in this point from earlier, however. A student, who doesn't show respect for the *Sensei*, shouldn't wonder if he doesn't carry on being trained by him.

Some *Sensei* retain the students' passes in their possession. If a student wants to attend a course, he has to ask the *Sensei* whether it is OK for him to do so. If the answer is affirmative then the *Sensei* registers the student for the course. There is no questioning of a traditionally oriented *Sensei* who turns it down – this simply has to be accepted. In my dojo, generally the students can go to all the courses. But the registration has to go over the *Sensei*. Registrations for grading tests also should flow through the *Sensei*. In other types of sport, such as for example Kali, the athletes can register themselves for the grading test. When a *Sensei*, or in Kali a Guro, tells a student that he shouldn't go for the test, and despite this the student goes ahead and registers himself, this is proof that the relationship between the *Sensei* and the student has broken down. In such a case the student will probably have to look for another new *Sensei* or *Guro*.

During the training session, work should go on with full concentration and in quietness. The partner should always be handled with respect and techniques executed in a controlled manner. If a student is not exercising then he should sit still on the edge of the mat. During an exercise when the one partner makes it known, by slapping the floor or shouting, that he gives in or that he is in pain, then the grip must be released immediately or the technique abandoned. A student lying around or lolling on the mat cannot be tolerated and can be punished by being excluded from the class.

The *Sensei's* instructions must be followed at all times. Furthermore, a student (even as a black belt holder) must not give any other student advice or lecturing, except when the *Sensei* tells him directly to do so. The exercises that have been laid down are the ones that should be carried out. Any other form of exercises that the student would like to execute is not permitted. If a student has to leave the hall (go to the toilet, injury, urgent telephone call) he should tell the *Sensei* quickly. As a basic rule, cell-phones should be switched off during the training session. In urgent cases (when on stand-by duty, calls from a babysitter etc.,) the *Sensei* will see good reason to relax his rules.

When a technique is being demonstrated, the student should position himself so that he can see everything. Retorts to the *Sensei* such as, "Turn round so I can see!" are simply not on and don't have much success anyway. Particularly so when the student is lying down somewhere chewing gum! Eating during the training session is not permitted, except where someone has an illness such as diabetes and this requires an exception.

Some *Sensei* also don't allow drinking during the training session. Others allow it, but it should not be done on the mat. When drinking the trainee should stand with his back to the mat. I organize short drink breaks in my training sessions, or let the group know early on when they can take a drink as they wish. But with some exercises it has a disturbing effect when the students are coming and going off the mat all the time, so I organize the drink breaks properly. Particularly in the summer months, I think it is very important to drink plenty, so I am quite relaxed about this point in the etiquette.

The third thing is cleanliness and hygiene. Not only should the clothing be clean, but also the body. About this I always remember a little story. I had a student, who always wore a light yellow Gi (tunic worn in Jiu-Jitsu, Judo and Karate etc.). After a few months, the student came to training with a white Gi. I asked him if he had bought himself a new outfit. His answer was negative, he had just washed his Gi. Gently, I asked him how often he washed his Gi, to which he replied that he washed it every 2-3 months. The Gi is soaked in sweat after a training session and therefore should be washed after every session. If a beginner has only one Gi and participates in several sessions during the week, he should at least wash it at the weekend so that it is fresh again for the next week's activities. If the session has not been particularly strenuous, then it is possible that it can be worn once again. As a rule I only wear my Gi once. My wife always says jokingly that if she had to chose a husband all over again then she would chose a swimmer, because swimwear doesn't have to be ironed, and washing and hanging it out is a lot easier.

The regulations lay down that the Jiu-Jitsu Gi has to be white. Ladies should wear a white T-shirt under it. Men don't wear T-shirts. Personally I don't mind if the male participants in my classes wear a T-shirt, but in most competitions it is forbidden to wear one. Especially in the winter months it can be very cold, and I can understand and agree that the men also want to wear one. As far as I am aware, in events lasting several days, the correct clothing must be worn at the first day's session and at the end of the last day. In the sessions in between, it's up to the referees to lay down the conditions. If throws aren't going to be carried out in the session, or they consider that a Gi is not necessary for a throw, then many referees will allow training exercises to be carried out wearing a T-shirt and trousers.

Also, many *Sensei* don't worry too much about the color of the Gi (blue, black, sometimes even green and red) in these interim periods. Personally, I think this relaxed approach is good. On the other hand, there are those that lay great value on having the correct clothing and etiquette all the time. Because of this, the trainee should ask the *Sensei* beforehand, what clothing rules he wants to lay down. Some *Sensei* also wear a blue Gi nowadays often saying that this serves to make it clear where he is on the mat. The wearing of another color is, however, not correct, but for now is merely tolerated. It should also be noted that only the badges of the club membership and perhaps the country's association and no others may be used to decorate the Gi tunic. In all cases, there should be no badge worn on the Gi, which represents any political background or tendency.

It is not only the Gi and belt that should be clean – the body should be also. Convention has it that before the trainee goes onto the mat he washes his feet, or if he is wearing appropriate footwear these are clean. Mat shoes are still not approved of much. There are, however, good reasons for them.

In diabetics, injuries to the feet do not heal well in many cases. If the student has a verruca, he should not be allowed to take part in the training, because of the great danger of contagion. In cases where there are injuries to the toes, the use of shoes is possible but rather difficult.

In this book, techniques from the Philippine martial arts (Arnis, Kali or Eskrima) have been included. Twenty years ago this was done using a mock rubber knife. Perhaps this training aid can be used in the Duo System fighting (less chance of injury).

It is difficult, if not impossible to lever a rubber knife out of the hands of a partner. For this, nowadays, an aluminum mock-up knife or sometimes a wooden one is used. It is quite unpleasant if an aluminum knife drops on the foot. Subsequently the athletes, who practice the Philippines system, often wear wrestling boots. This type of footwear for the mat have been seen worn also at many Jiu-Jitsu events. It is wise, however, in this case or at least before training starts, to clear up the position with the *Sensei* to find out his attitude towards them being worn and whether he will allow it.

Finger and toenails should be cut so that they will cause no injuries to your partner. The ladies should take their makeup off before training, or at least make sure that it won't dirty or stain the partner's clothing. I, myself, had a terrible problem once when exercising with a lady, who was heavily made up, and it took me a lot of effort to get the coloring out of my suit afterwards. Even new, colored suits should be washed several times before the first use in training to avoid the colors running onto the lighter colored suits of the others. I have seen some good examples of this problem too. Jewelry should be left at home. Sometimes it's not possible to remove for example an earring in an earlobe that has just been pierced, and this should be plastered over. Despite plastering there is also a heightened danger of injury. The *Sensei* will lay down what is to be done in such cases. Some *Sensei* insist that the student stays away from training until the piece of jewelry can be properly removed. When ground-fighting, there is a high risk of danger to the ears, especially if an earring is being worn, and the word of the *Sensei* is best followed in these cases.

The fourth and last area is loyalty to the trainer, the club and the national association. For example, in Germany – the home country of the author – if another martial arts association has been declared as competition for the German Ju-Jutsu Association (GJJA), then any member of the GJJA will be expected to stay away from events held by the other association. Otherwise that person can expect repercussions from his own association if he doesn't. A student should always remember who taught him and stand by his trainer or trainers. As already mentioned, it is not common that students sign up for courses on their own. According to etiquette, it is normally laid down that the student has to get the approval of his trainer. This is the same for taking tests or for the participation in a training session in another association or school. Prior clarification of the situation with the *Sensei*, helps also in such cases in avoiding differences.

Many of the items mentioned are not workable for a person who is only following the art as a pure leisure sport. A martial art, whether it stems from the Japanese, the Philippines or the Spanish systems (the list is merely an example), has numerous different rules. Notwithstanding this, many other types of sports have similar points of etiquette. For example, in national football matches, the players line up and after the national anthems have been played, the players all shake hands before they start the game. This is also an item of etiquette.

Most trainers in the martial arts are not well rewarded in comparison to other types of sports. So as a result, they expect a student to have sufficient self-discipline to come to training regularly, be willing to learn and always try to improve himself. Irregular and late attendance at training is often followed up by a punishment.

As a *Sensei*, I often take problems, that cannot be solved in training, 'home' with me; e.g., there was once a problem with a student who simply was unable to execute a certain technique. Sometime, in the middle of the night, the solution came to me suddenly and I would have loved to have gone straight away to the dojo to solve the problem.

The relationship between the *Sensei* and a 'proper' student is like a father/son or father/daughter relationship. After a few years of training the 'children' grow up and have their own ideas, which they want to include in their training. However, it is advisable that the "young grown-up" has a chat with "Dad" first so that there will be no arguments.

TECHNICAL SECTION

1 INTRODUCTION

When I started Jiu-Jitsu, twenty years ago, the complete series of the breakfall (front and back breakfall, fall sideways, foreflap and backwards) as well as all the active blocking techniques (forearm block outwards, inwards, upwards, down and outwards and down and inwards) were taught.

Nowadays, at the beginning of breakfall training, I teach only the sideways fall as this is the breakfall, which a competing martial arts athlete needs the most. Following on from this I teach the passive blocking techniques. Then, later on, I teach the forwards and backwards roll as well as the active blocks. The reason for this is that to be able to do these techniques successfully, certain in-built reflex reactions have to be present. The reason for learning the passive blocks first is that these reflect the human, natural instincts where, for example, you automatically protect your head or your body with an arm whenever someone is trying to injure you with a punch or a kick. Basic forms of movement such as postures/stances, evading actions and step turns are also taught.

For a few years, now, fights without (or with very few) rules are carried out. In these competitions, fighters from different styles meet against each other. The upshot of these fights is that a fighter without qualified training in ground-fighting has only a slim chance. A member of the Gracie family, who followed the Gracie Jiu-Jitsu style, had great success in this for a long while. The specialty in this form is ground-fighting. Similarly, many fighters with knowledge of the Luta-Livre were very successful in ground-fighting. Because of the importance of ground-fighting abilities, many martial arts systems have broadened their style to take on these techniques. Also other sports styles such as Wing Tsun (has also other spellings) have at least brought in "anti ground-fighting", although it used to be assumed that a trained fighter didn't go in for ground-fighting.

I have also included the ground-fighting techniques in my series of books so that there is a central thread running through them of immobilizing techniques, freeing techniques, as well as the execution of the final techniques. In this book, here, the technique is shown how the student can immobilize an opponent or react to his counter-movements by shifting his weight in ground-fighting.

Carrying on, I go on to show preliminary locking and Atemi techniques (punching and kicking) that can stop an attack developing. One of these techniques is the stomping kick – a very effective technique quite capable of warding off an attack. This kick can also be found in Wing Tsun (also spelled differently). Instead of using a normal fist punch, a chain of punches can be used. This technique also stems from Wing Tsun or Jeet Kune Do. It is also a very effective technique and, if carried out properly, it is very difficult to defend against.

If the counter and continuation techniques were earlier held back from those practicing Jiu-Jitsu, then the basics can be found in this work. The student can learn how to avoid the start of a throw and how he can best carry on after his locking technique has been blocked.

In the section on "Free Self-defense", the student can learn about defense against contact attacks (different grip methods) using free combinations. The attacks are those in the Duo-Series 1. The Duo Competition Fighting system, used world wide, contains a series of predetermined attacks. In this system, pairs of competitors come against each other to show off their defensive techniques. This competition system is also interesting for the layman, because it is optically very pleasing. In the past, however, no great value was laid on the most effective techniques, rather attention was only paid to other points, which I don't wish to go into here at this juncture. I find the Duo system competition particularly interesting for children, because now they can measure how good their combinations are in comparison to other people. This is without the danger of injuring themselves as possible in normal sparring competitions (as in e.g., the Fighting-System).

A further section takes the student on to the actual fight during the course of his training. In the section "Free Applications", we gradually raise the complexity until, after successful instruction, the student can hold his own with throws, punching and kicking techniques, both in a standing and a ground position. In the first section, the initial exercises are done with the open hand standing. The aim is for the student to be able to strike the opponent with the open hand (without hurting him), to be able to move about effectively and to avoid being struck himself.

Many of the combinations that I have selected are, in my opinion, very demanding for the beginner. However, my philosophy is to teach these techniques as early on as possible, even if the combinations are sometimes very complex. I have also taken the trouble to build in several, which are simpler in their movement sequence, so that the most appropriate ones can be sought out for the student according to his talent or previous knowledge.

As a basic marker – in the following chapters the defender is indicated by the letter 'D' and the attacker/opponent 'A'.

2 STANCES

2.1 FROM A DEFENSE POSTURE BY USING AN EXTENSION MOVEMENT INTO TWO DIFFERENT FORMS OF ACTION STANCES

- Starting posture   • Offensive form

2.1.1 Offensive Form of the Action Stance

- Extension of the defensive posture forwards and outwards.

- Moving the body weight in the direction of the forward leg (approximately 30% to 70%).

- Distinctly dropping the center of gravity of the body.

- Application mainly used in connection with Atemi techniques.

- Starting posture
- Defensive form

2.1.2 Defensive Form of the Action Stance

- Extension of the defensive posture to the rear

- Moving the body weight in the direction of the rear leg (approximately 60% to 40%).

- Slightly dropping the center of gravity of the body.

- Application mainly used in connection with defensive techniques

3   Forms of Movement (Sabaki)

3.1   Changing Stances

- Forwards

- On the spot

- Starting position

- Rearwards

3.2 Dodging Movements

3.2.1 Weaving

- To the rear

- To the side

3.2.2 Ducking Down

3.2.3 Weaving and Ducking Down

3.3   Gliding

Backwards

Sideways

Starting position

3.4. Maintaining Body Cover

Forwards

3.5   STEP TURNS

3.5.1   90° STEP TURN
- Rearwards
- Starting Position
- Forwards

3.5.2   180° STEP TURN
- Forwards
- Rearwards

3.6 LUNGE STEP

Lunge step forwards   Lunge step backwards

Sideways lunge step (right and left)

Diagonal lunge step forwards (right and left)

Diagonal lunge step backwards (right and left)

3.7 Double Step Turns

Double step turn 90°

Double step turn 180°

Double step turn 180° (into a parallel standing stance)

4 Breakfalls (Ukemi)

4.1 Falling on the Side

4.2   Falling to the Rear on the Back

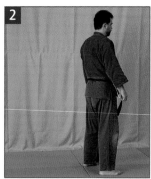

4.3   Forward-roll

5 Groundwork Techniques (Ne-waza)

5.1 Hold-down Technique in a Sideways Position (Kesa-Gatame)

- The opponent is on his back. Defender is positioned by his side.
- One arm is holding on to the opponent's arm closest to the defender.
- The other arm is holding the head or the opponent's other arm.
- The leg nearest the ground is pinning the shoulder nearest to the defender.
- The opponent is kept pinned down by exerting pressure on his body.

5.2 Hold-down Technique with Crossover of the Body (Yoko-Shio-Gatame)

- Opponent is on his back. The defender is laying crosswise over his body.
- Both arms are holding the opponent's head and/or arms.
- The opponent is kept pinned down by keeping the pressure on his body.

5.3   Hold-down Technique in the Straddle Position (Tate-Shiho-Gatame)

- Opponent is on his back. The defender is sitting straddling the opponent's body.

- Both arms are holding the opponent's head and/or arms.

- The defender's knees and feet block the opponent's hips.

- The opponent is kept pinned down by keeping the pressure on his body.

5.4 Escape from Hold-down Techniques

- It is up to the student what freeing technique he should use from any hold-down, and the necessary grip-holds on his partner that he uses to achieve this.
- The action of freeing is successful when the defender manages to do a turnover and hold-down the attacker, or when he can free himself from the attacker's grip.
- Freeing is also counted when there is not enough resistance applied by the attacker.

In defense, groundwork plays a big role when reacting to the pressure and position of the attacker's body. It is very important to realize where the attacker's central point of gravity is. This is what freeing is all about. While mass is an important criterion when fighting in the standing position, in groundwork, this attribute is even more important. If two people are technically equal, the heavier fighter will always have an advantage. It is important in training to take time first of all to practice the pure techniques without any resistance being applied. After a while, practice can be carried out with light defensive resistance being applied, working up later to full defense in a fighting mode or in competition. Constant control of the extremities of the partner's body is the main point to which attention must be paid. Merely a pure Judo type of defense should be avoided. In Judo, you do not punch or kick, and while freeing can often be easily achieved, it is neglected to remember that the attacker could be using punching, biting and kicking techniques.

5.4.1 Escape from a Hold-down Technique in a Sideways Position (from a Kesa-Gatame)

1. A is lying on the side against D with his center of gravity held forwards. The rear (left) leg is placed a little to the side.

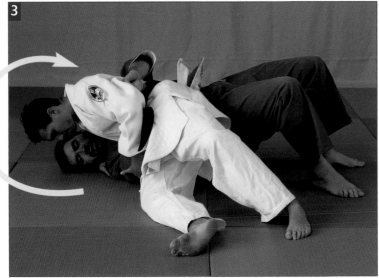

2. D lies over onto his right side and grabs round A's stomach with his left arm. He then tries (important!) to free his right arm from A's grip and pull it down so that he is lying on the ground. D pulls both of his feet up near to his bottom and now D holds A closely and firmly.

3. D lifts up his hips and first of all pulls A in the direction of his right shoulder.

4. After that he rolls over on his shoulder blades and brings A onto his left side...

5. ...so that now he is in the sideways position.

1. A is lying on his side on D and has both of his legs stretched out with his upper body upright.

2. D moves his legs to the left to get at an approximate angle of 180° in line to A.

3. After that, D pushes his body forward, thus causing A to fall over backwards...

4. ...and so, comes into the sideways position himself.

1. A is lying sideways against D and has his rear, left leg stretched right out to support himself.
2. D lies over on to the right side of his body, gets hold of A's upper body with both arms.
3. He moves his left leg over A's rear, left leg and brings his right leg under A's left leg...
4. ...and turns A to the left
5. ...and so, now he is in the sideways position himself.

5.4.2 ESCAPE FROM A CONTROL TECHNIQUE WITH CROSSOVER OF THE Body (FROM THE Yoko-Shio-Gatame)

1. A is lying on D with the weight of his body over the left upper half of D's body.
2. D brings both of his feet on the floor up to his bottom and 'bucks' (sharp upward movement of the hips) A upwards,...
3. ...and as he sinks down again lies over onto his left side, bringing his right hand onto the right-hand side of A's head and grabs the head. D pulls A's head

down in the direction of the ground...

4.-5. and scrabbles clockwise round A...

6. ...until he gets into the crossover position himself.

1. A is lying on D with the weight of his body over the right upper half of D's body.
2. D brings both of his feet on the floor up to his bottom, and 'bucks' (sharp upward movement of the hips) A upwards,...
3. ...and as he sinks down again lies over onto his right side, grabbing A's left thigh with both hands/arms...
4. ...and pulls this inwards and places the weight of his upper body onto A's upper body...
5. ...so that A falls over backwards.

1. A is lying on D with the weight of his body over the upper half of D's body. D places both feet on the floor up to his bottom...
2. ...and 'bucks' (sharp upward movement of the hips) A upwards,...
3. ...and before he sinks down again, he brings his right forearm towards A's groin, so that D has more room. D brings his right arm in front of A's right arm i.e., he is now blocking A's right arm.
4. After this, D places his right arm between A's legs and scrabbles anti-clockwise round A to the left...
5. ...pulls his legs back in and lifts his hips up...
6. ...to turn A onto his back.

5.4.3 Escaping from a Control Technique in the Straddle Position (from the Tate-Shiho-Gatame)

1. A is sitting on D holding his lapels in both hands.
2. D rips A's right hand down to his chest with his left hand.
3. After this, D lays the palm of his right hand behind A's right elbow, so that A cannot pull it out of the blocking movement. D blocks A's foot/lower leg using his left foot by placing it next to A's foot/leg. The right foot is placed close up to his own bottom.

4. The hips are jerked upwards and he turns A over the left shoulder onto his back.

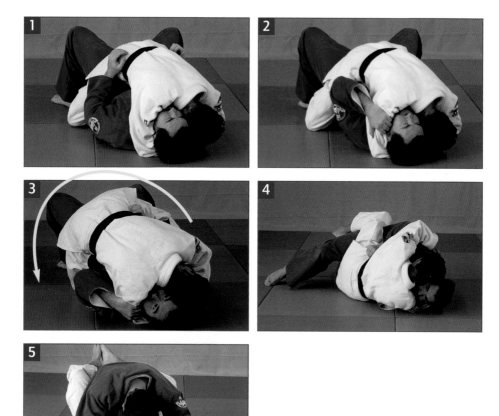

1. A is sitting on D in the straddle position with his right arm underneath D's neck e.g., as if to start a neck lift/stranglehold.
2. D blocks A's right arm with his left arm, so that he cannot pull it out from underneath D's head. D presses his head down onto the ground so that A cannot pull his arm out from here also. D blocks A's right foot/lower leg with his right foot by placing it against A's foot/leg. The right foot is placed close up to his own bottom. D places his right hand on A's left hip,...
3. ...jerks his hips upwards...
4.-5. ...and turns A over the left shoulder onto his back.

6   Complex Exercise

6.1   Demonstration of Fist Techniques on a Moving but Passive Partner

- Both partners are moving around at middle reach from each other.

- One of them has to attack the other with all kinds of fist techniques.

- If only light contact is made this does not count.

- The partner may only move about, do dodges and passive defensive movements.

- Points will be scored:
  For economic and controlled movement,
  execution of correct techniques, timing,
  good feeling for the reach, good
  overview and dynamics.

7 Jiu-Jitsu Combination Techniques

The following techniques should be carried out using combinations against each type of attack.

The combinations illustrated in this book are only examples and serve to encourage those interested.

7.1 Defensive Techniques (Uke-waza)

7.1.1 Passive Defense Techniques Blocking with the Forearm (Uke-Waza)

- The forearm nearest the head or the body is the one which protects that area against a strike.
- The defense technique should be combined with the appropriate form of movement.

7.1.1.1 At Head Height (Outside)

1. D defends with a passive, left-cover block upwards and outwards.
2. D's left arm is slipped over A's striking arm and pressed into his lumbar region while his right hand is brought up from below to deliver an open-palm strike.

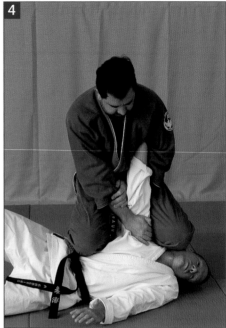

3. D does a 45° lunge step forward to the left and foot-trips A down onto the ground by placing his right leg behind A's right leg, turning his body and pressing with his right hand against A's chin to make him fall.
4. D ends the combination using an inside stretched arm lock to hold down, kneeling with both knees on A. The left knee is on A's neck and the right knee on his lower chest.

1. D defends with a passive, left-cover block upwards and outwards.
2. D brings A's striking arm by using the three-step contact (Hubud) from above to the inside: First, slide the right hand under A's right arm.
3. With the right hand bring A's arm to the inside and grab his right wrist, placing the left forearm on A's right elbow...
4. ...and bring A down to the ground with a stretched arm lock.
5. D places his left knee between A's shoulder blades and executes a wrist lock to immobilize him.

1. D executes a passive block upwards and outwards simultaneously delivering a strike with the ball of the right hand to the chin.
2. Followed by a variation of the two-handed crescent sweep like e.g., taught in the Luta-Livre; D kneels on his right knee in front of A having placed his left leg next to A's right leg. D grabs round both legs at the height of the hollows of the knees and pulls them together so they form an 'X'.
3. By pressing against the legs D causes A to fall...
4. ...and then goes immediately into the cross-over position.
5. He ends the combination with a bent arm lock.

7.1.1.2 At Middle Body Height (Outside)

1. D stands in a defensive position with both arms held up covering.
   A carries out an uppercut at the lower rib cage and D pulls his left arm closer into the body (passive block downwards and outwards) to protect the lower rib cage.

2. D brings his right hand from the inside round A's nape of the neck and pulls A's body forwards. At the same time, D executes a knee kick to A's upper body.

3. After this, his left hand goes up from below A's right arm and he lays it on the elbow and executes a turning stretched arm lock...

4. ...and pulls A down further forwards to get him on to his stomach.

5. D kneels from A's head onto the attacker, grabs both of his arms, pulls them up and executes a shoulder lock. (Note: It looks like a stretched arm lock, but because there is no pressure placed on the elbow joint, the main pressure is on the shoulder joint.)

1. D stands in a defensive position with both arms held up covering.
   A carries out an uppercut at the lower rib cage and D pulls his left arm closer into the body (passive block) to protect the lower rib cage, executing at the same time a right-handed punch at the chin.

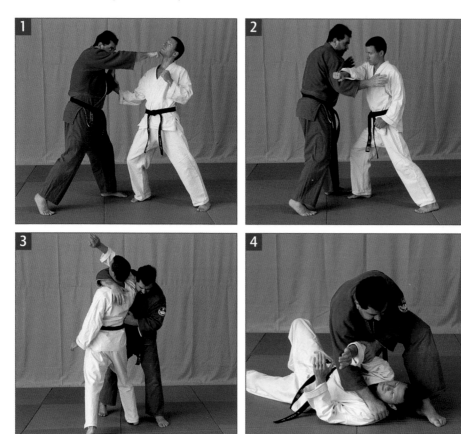

2. D brings A's striking arm downwards and inwards by using the three-step contact: The blocking technique has already occurred by virtue of the passive block, now the right arm is brought over A's attacking right arm and then swept downwards and inwards (counterclockwise) past D.
3. D brings his own right arm further upwards and places his arm from the left side of the neck round A's neck. As he does this he goes forward with a 45° step and presses his left fist into A's right kidney so that A is forced to arch his back. As he does this both of D's arms are pointing in the direction of A's arms.

4. D makes A fall over backwards.
5. D presses A's face in the direction of his left side with his left hand, and holds it on the face, holding and controlling A's right arm with his own right hand.
6. D steps over A's head with his left leg.
7. D brings his other leg over A's stomach and ends the combination with a stretched arm lock in the crossover position.

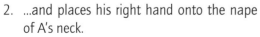

1. D stands in a defensive position with both arms held up covering. A carries out an uppercut at the lower rib cage and D pulls his left arm closer into the body (passive block) to protect the lower rib cage, and at the same time he 'rubs' his right thumb over A's left eye...

2. ...and places his right hand onto the nape of A's neck.

3. D now pulls A's head under his left armpit so that the back of D's right hand is lying directly under his left armpit.

4. D brings his left arm round A's head and grabs his own right wrist and starts a choke/stranglehold technique with his arms (guillotine). D pulls his knees closely together (in self-defense against punches and kicks to the genital area) and stretches himself so that pressure is brought onto the nape of the neck.

7.1.1.3 At Middle Body Height (Inside)

1. A executes a thumb strike into the solar plexus.
2. D counters with a passive block to the inside, at the same time grabbing the right side of A's nape of the neck with his right hand.
3. D executes a right-legged knee kick against A's right thigh.
4. With his left hand, D pulls A's right arm to the inside so that A's right leg is unweighted and then does a right-footed sweep to the rear.

5. A is now on all fours with his right leg stretched out. Now D positions himself at the right hand of A and delivers two kicks with his right leg to A's thigh/hips or the ribs.

1. A tries to push D backwards by pushing with both arms. With his left arm D makes a passive block to the inside...
2. ...brings the arm down and further outwards...
3. ...and brings A's right arm into a twisting stretched arm lock.
4. He then delivers a right-legged knee kick at A's head...
5. ...and brings him down with twist throw...
6. ...gets into the straddle position, hooks both of his legs under A's legs. He then lays his right arm under the nape of A's neck and then holds on to his left biceps. He places his left hand on A's forehead, while A lays his face on the back of D's hand. The right shoulder is in front of A's chin. D pushes himself forwards and ends the combination with neck lock.

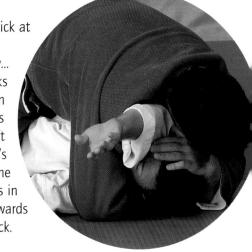

1. A delivers a kick forwards with his right foot at D's stomach.
   D executes an inside passive block with his left arm and covers his head with his right arm in case A tries to counter with a backhand strike.
2. D does a sideways lunge step to the left with his left leg.
   Right-footed kick with the shinbone (low kick) to the front of the thigh.
3. Simultaneously, a left jab to the head.
4. Right uppercut to the chin.
5. D places his left leg to the rear and delivers a shinbone kick to the front of A's thigh.

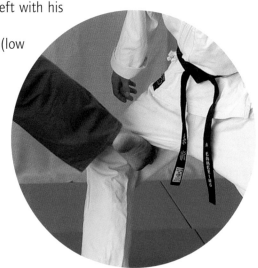

7.1.2 Active Defense Techniques Blocking with the Forearm (Uke-Waza)

- The defense is done using the inside edge of the forearm (ulna) or the outside edge of the forearm (radius).
- The hand of the defending arm can be used open or closed.
- The defensive techniques should be combined with the appropriate forms of movement.

7.1.2.1 To the Inside

1. A executes a knife attack sweeping in from above down to the inside.
2. D counters with a left forearm block to the inside and simultaneously gets hold of A's wrist with his right hand so that he cannot pull it back.

3. Using the right hand the wrist is forced downwards and inside until the tip of the knife is pointing at the ground. The ball of the opponent's thumb is gripped hard as this is done.

4.-5. D continues disarming the opponent by using his own left hand to lever the knife away – (as he disarms, the palm of D's left hand is pointing up at the ceiling and the inside edge of the hand is placed along the flat, blunt side of the knife).

1. A strikes towards D's head with a backhand hit.
2. D counters by using a forearm block to the inside. His right hand is protecting his face and stops the striking hand so that it cannot be pulled back.
3. Using his left hand, D brings A's right arm downwards and outwards to the left...
4. ...using a twisting stretched arm lock. His right hand presses A's head downwards 45° so that A cannot grab D's legs.

5. D swings his left leg over A's head
6. and throws him to the ground with a twisting throw.
7.-8. D moves into the straddle position holding A's right arm as he does...
9. ...and slips his right knee over A's left arm...
10. ...places his left foot directly next to the left side of A's head – his toes are pointing forwards – and executes a stretched arm lock over the left groin.

1.-2. A executes a right-footed kick forwards at D's stomach. D carries out a 90° step turn backwards, while at the same time doing a left forearm block downwards and inwards. His right hand is protecting his own head.

3. This is followed up with an open-handed punch with his right hand at A's head.

4. D places his left leg back rearwards...

5. ...and ends the combination with a shinbone kick to the rear side of the left thigh.

7.1.2.2 To the Outside

1. A executes a knife attack sweeping in up to the right to the outside of D's neck. D counters with a left forearm block to the outside and simultaneously delivers an open-handed jab at A's eyes with his right hand.

2.-4. Using the right hand, A's hand holding the weapon is brought upwards and outwards...

5. ...until the tip of the knife is pointing at the ground. The opponent's right hand thumb is gripped hard using the right hand as this is done (in order to open A's grip). The left forearm is placed on the flat, broad side.

6. Using the left forearm, pressure is applied forwards and the knife is levered out of the hand.

7. D now places his left forearm on A's right forearm, and with his right arm he pulls A's right arm making a sharp 45° tug downwards with his left arm (this brings A quickly forwards). In connection with this, here, D could execute a direct head strike on A.

8. D's right hand grabs A's neck laying his left hand on A's lower back...

9.-10. ...and brings A down to the ground by bending his body over.

11. D grabs A's wrist with his left hand and his right hand on A's elbow.

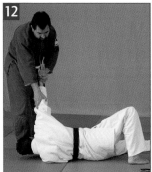

12.-13. Pulling on the hand and with pressure on the elbow, A is turned over onto his stomach.

14.   D places his right leg over A's right arm and wraps his arm round A's right leg.

15.   Using a crossover bent arm lock round the leg, D ends the combination.

1. A executes an in-swinging punch with his left fist. D counters with a right-handed forearm block outwards.
2. A executes a second in-swinging punch with his right fist. D counters with a left-handed forearm block outwards.
3. D grabs hold of A's head with both hands...
4. ...and executes a head butt...
5. ...followed by a two-handed crescent sweep like e.g., taught in the Luta-Livre; D kneels on his right knee in front of A having placed his

left leg next to of A's right leg. D grabs round both legs at the height of the hollows of the knees and pulls them together so they form an 'X'.

6. Using pressure on his legs, D causes A to fall backwards...
7. ...and immediately goes into the straddle hold position.
8. He ends the combination with a bent arm lock.

1.-2. A executes a front kick at D's stomach. D counters with a right-handed forearm block downwards and outwards, simultaneously protecting his head covering with his left hand.

3. D takes a circular step backwards with his left foot...

4.-6. ...pulls A off-balance by applying pressure on to his left shoulder and executes a right roundhouse.

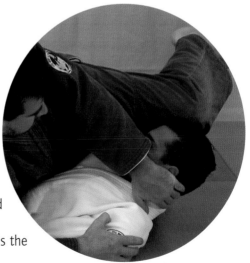

7. D goes down into the side position. For this, A's right arm is clamped between the right side of his body and his right thigh.
The left hand gets hold of A's head around its left-hand side.

8. A left-legged knee kick at A's head ends the combination.

7.1.3 Defense Techniques Blocking with the Hand (Uke-Waza)

- In defense the flat, tensed hand is used.
- Execution is by choice, with either the flat of the hand, the back of the hand, the outside edge of the hand, the inside edge of the hand or the ball of the hand.
- The defense technique should be combined with the appropriate form of movement.

7.1.3.1 Technique: Sweeping Hand

1. A executes a straight, right-handed punch at D's head.
   D counters with a sweep of the left hand to the inside (the fingers are closed!)...
2. ...and 'curls' his left hand clockwise round A's upper arm.
3. At the same time, his right hand grabs the nape of A's neck.
4. D executes a kick with his right foot at A's left knee...
5. ...and brings A down with twisting stretched arm lock onto the ground and uses this technique as an immobilizing grip.

1. A executes a strike with a stick upwards and from the inside.
2. D wards off the strike of the stick downwards to the left and to the outside by using the back of his hand (fingers are closed)...
3.-4. ...and disarms A using the "snake" disarming movement.
5. D places his left hand under the right triceps and executes a strike with the right elbow against the right biceps (gunting technique).
6. The right hand folds over downwards and brings A's right arm to the right and outside. He follows this up with a left-fisted punch at A's right kidney.
7. After this, D rubs his right thumb over A's right eye...
8. ...and concludes with a left-fisted punch at A's chin.

1. A executes a right-handed knife attack upwards and outwards towards D's neck.
2. D sweeps the arm with the knife diagonally down to the right and outwards using the right hand (with the fingers closed).
3. D brings his left hand underneath A's right elbow and pushes his right hand or his right arm over A's right arm (to control the arm holding the weapon). As he does this, he also delivers a finger/hand jab towards A's eyes.
4. D slips his right hand along the right arm and grabs hold of the ball of the right hand...
5. ...brings the hand inside past his own left arm with his right hand...
   ...stretches the left arm out...
   ...lays the blunt, flat side of the knife onto the left biceps...
6. ...pulls the right hand over his own left biceps and thus disarms A.
7. Using his left arm D rolls it over A's right arm...
8. ...and lays it down on A's right elbow and applies a stretched arm lock.

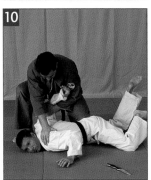

9. D brings A down to the ground by applying pressure on the stretched arm lock...

10. ...and in the ground position, he angles A's right arm round his own left arm...
    ...and using his right hand, he traps A's left shoulder blade (so that A cannot turn over and execute an elbow strike)...
    ...and applies pressure with his left against A's levered upper arm...

11. ...forcing A to move forwards and stand up...

12. ...and then executes a cross-armed grip (bent arm lock to move A about).

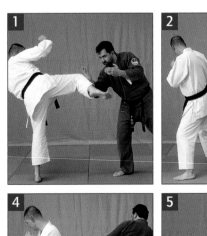

1. A executes a semi-circular front kick with his right foot at D's upper body.
    D grabs hold of the attacking leg with his right hand (hand sweep)...

2. ...and directs the foot to the outside...
3. ...so that A is now standing with his back to D.
4. D executes a kick with his left shinbone 45° upwards at the rear of A's right thigh...
5. ...and grabs hold of A's head with both hands...
6. ...'jumps' round the attacker and executes a knee kick to his head,...
7.-8. ...executes a knife-hand strike at A's head with his right hand with which he ends the combination.

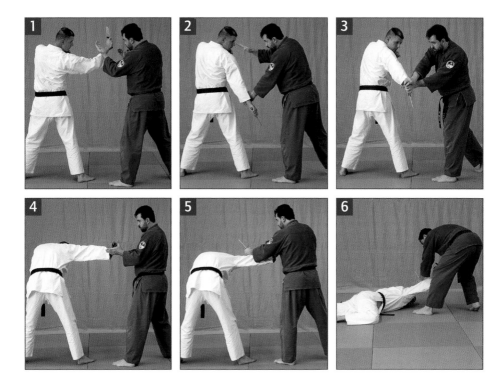

1. A executes a knife attack upwards to the inside of D's neck.
2. D counters with a spear-hand jab at A's eyes with his right hand, at the same time doing a diagonal sweeping block with his left hand (the fingers are closed).
3. D's right hand grabs hold of A's right hand...
4. ...and pulls it inwards to effect an inward turning bent wrist lock.
5. The left hand removes the knife.
6. D executes a stretched arm lock to bring A down to the ground and immobilizes him likewise.

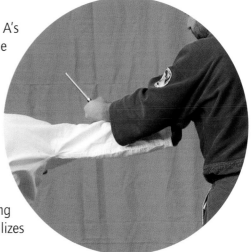

1. A executes an attack with a pistol touching D's chest with it.
2. D counters by doing a left-handed sweeping block to the inside.
3. D turns the weapon in A's direction and can either do a wrist lock or a disarming action.
4. D pulls it further outwards to the left and disarms A.
5. A punch with the weapon at A's head ends the combination.

1. A executes a knife attack upwards at D's head.
2. D does a left-handed sweeping block downwards and at the same time he executes an open-fingered jab with his right hand at A's eyes.
3. D grabs the ball of the thumb from underneath with his right hand and opens A's grip.
4.-5. D takes the knife out of A's hand with his left hand.
6. D places his left leg to the rear...
7. ...and ends the combination with semi-circular roundhouse kick at A's head or a shinbone kick at his thigh.

7.1.3.2 Technique: Using the shoulder block

1. A executes a right-handed punch (cross punch) at D's head.
    D counters using a right-arm shoulder block on A's right shoulder.
    As he does this he covers his head with his left hand.
2.-3. D executes a twisting throw by:
    *   Grabbing the nape of the neck on the inside with his right hand.
    *   Bringing A's right arm upwards using his left arm.
    *   Turning A's head inwards with his right hand and bringing it up to the point of A's elbow

  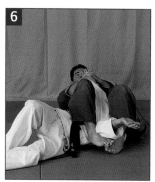

4.-5. D brings A's head further towards the inside and throws him with a twisting throw down to the ground.

6.   He ends the combination using a crossover stretched arm lock.

1.   A executes a right-handed punch (cross punch) at D's head.
      D counters using a right-armed shoulder block on A's right shoulder, covering his head with his left hand.

2.   D executes a left-handed punch (cross punch)...

3.-4. ...and a hammer punch with his right fist at the left side of A's neck,

5.   ...places his left leg one pace to the left and rearwards...

6.   ...and ends the combination with a right-legged shinbone kick at the front of A's thigh.

1. A executes a strike with a stick coming in down from the right,

D counters with a right-arm shoulder block, covering his own face with his left hand.

2.-3. D brings the stick hand downwards and outwards with his right hand...

4. ...and swaps over to his left hand holding the stick hand by the wrist...

5.-6. ...and disarms him with his right forearm...

7. D "rolls" his right arm along A's right arm and grabs hold of A holding him by the right side of his chest...

8.-9. ...getting round behind A as he does. With his right hand he grabs hold of A's left lapel and with his left arm he grabs hold round A's neck and executes a stranglehold by pulling on both the lapel and the neck at the same time.

7.2   Atemi Techniques

7.2.1   Palm Heel Techniques (Teisho-uchi, Teisho-tsuki)

- Atemi techniques using the palm heel of the hand.
- The striking surface is the heel of the palm, the hand being angled backwards sharply just prior to the strike going in.
- The fingers are slightly bent as the strike occurs.
- Straight-armed punches and cross punches are both possible.

7.2.1.1 Cross Punches

1. A delivers a clip on the ear against D's head with his right fist.
    D counters using a left forearm block outwards, then grips the attacking arm over the top of it and grabs the triceps.

2.　D executes a right-handed palm heel strike round from the right at A's chin.
3.　His right hand grabs A's left shoulder.
4.-5. Leg trip.
6.　Straight punch to the head as a final technique.

1. A executes a knife attack coming in from the right at D's head.
2. D counters with a left forearm block outwards.
3. D executes a right-handed palm heel strike at A's head and at the same time twists A's right hand counterclockwise and downwards.

4. D grabs the ball of the thumb of A's right hand in order to prize open the grip on the knife...
5.-7. ...and removes it with his left hand.

1. A carries out a stranglehold grip on D's throat at the same time delivering a clip on the ear with his left fist.
2. D pulls his shoulders up to make it difficult for A to complete the stranglehold. D pulls A's right arm down slightly with his left hand
3. and blocks A's attacking arm with his right arm (passive block).
4. D executes a right-fisted palm heel strike at A's chin...
5. ...brings his own right arm over A's right arm and does a bent arm lock.
6. D's left hand pushes A's face round counterclockwise to the rear.
7. D throws A onto the ground with a neck lock.
8. D ends the combination with a straight punch at A's head.

7.2.1.2 Palm Heel Strike

1. A executes a front kick at D's upper body. D counters with an inside passive block...
2. ...combined with a 90° step turn backwards.
3. Then D delivers a palm heel strike at A's head.

4. D places his left leg a little to the rear...
5. ...and executes a right shinbone kick (low-kick) at the rear of A's left thigh.
6. D continues turning counterclockwise...
7. ...and places his left leg behind A's left leg.
8. By sweeping away A's leg, D brings him down to the ground.

1. A executes a right-handed knife attack down at D's neck.
2. D counters by doing a diagonal hand sweep downwards and outwards with his right hand, and...
3. ...grabs hold of A's elbow with his left hand...
4. ...while delivering a palm heel strike at A's head with his right hand.
5. D pulls his right hand back again and grips the ball of the thumb of A's right hand. In this way A's grip is freed.
6. D brings A's right hand clockwise downwards so that the tip of the knife is pointing down at the ground.
7. D places the inside edge of his left hand along the broad blunt side of the knife and disarms A by levering the weapon forward out of A's hand with his left hand.

7.2.2 LUNGING PUNCH TECHNIQUES (Oi-tsuki, Gyaku-tsuki)

- The fist must be delivered to the target in a straight line.
- Possible ways of carrying out the punch:
  As a single punch with much of the impetus gathered from the hips and with the striking surface composed of the joints of the forefinger and middle finger, or...
  As a repeated punching series gaining impetus from the center of the body and with the striking surface composed of all of the joints from the forefinger to the little finger.

1. A executes a right-legged shinbone kick (low kick) at D's thigh. D counters by starting a knee block against A's shinbone.
2.-4. Then comes the series of straight blasts (several – one after the other) at A's face.
5. D rubs both thumbs over A's eyes...
6. ...grabs A's neck...
7. ... and delivers a head butt at A...
8. ...D delivers a knee kick at A's genitalia.

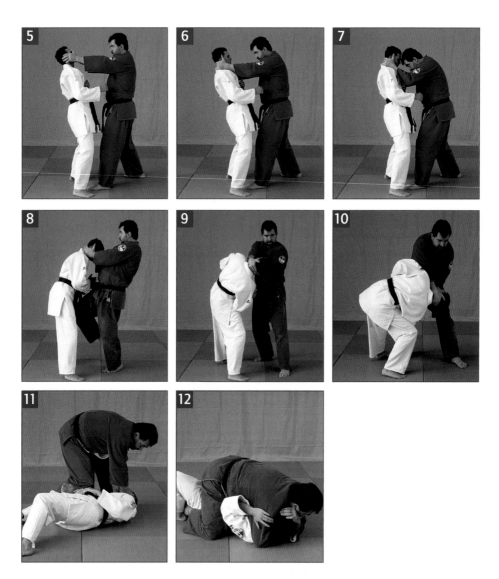

9.-11. D pulls A's body further down in the direction of the ground.

12. D adopts the straddle position, hooks both of his legs under A's, brings his right forearm under A's neck, places his right hand onto his own left biceps, places his left hand on A's face and the right half of the face on to the back of his own right hand, and then pushes the right shoulder under A's chin. By bringing the body forwards, firstly it increases the pressure on the neck lock and secondly brings pressure onto the jawbone using the shoulder.

1. With his left foot leading, A executes a right-fisted, straight punch (cross) at the head.
   D counters with a right arm passive block (salute-block).
2. Then does a left hook with his left fist at A's chin...
3. ...and a right-fisted punch (cross) to the stomach.
4. D places his left foot to the rear...
5. ...and ends the combination with a shinbone kick (low kick) at A's forward leg.

1. A executes a left-fisted punch (jab) leading with his left foot. D carries out a sweeping right arm block towards the inside.

2. A executes a second, right-fisted punch (cross). D counters again by carrying out a sweeping, this time left arm block...

3. ...and then a punch at the chin with his right fist...

4.-6. ...followed by a double leg takedown; D kneels on his right knee in front of A having placed his left leg next to A's right leg. D grabs round both legs at the height of the hollows of the knees and pulls them together so they form an 'X'. By pressing against the legs D makes A fall over backwards...

7. ...and moves into the side position.
8. D leads A's right arm over his neck.
9. With his head he presses against the right upper arm (around the height of the shoulder), grabs round underneath the neck with his right arm and grabs hold of his own right wrist with his left hand. D lies directly alongside A and executes a stranglehold with his arms.

7.2.3 Punch Techniques (Age-tsuki, Mawashi-tsuki, Uraken-uchi)

- The fist is brought on to the target in a semicircle.
- There are vital areas open in any direction.
- Possible ways of carrying out the punch:
  As a hook or backfist punch (with striking surface being the joints of the fore- and middle finger), or, as a hammer punch with the striking surface being the side of the fist where the little finger is.

1. A grabs hold of both wrists in a forward stance.
2. D counters by breaking the grip on the left wrist, done by bringing his own left elbow up to the attacker's right elbow.
3. D executes a left backfist at A's nose...

4. ...and bends his left arm inwards and downwards, thus blocking A's left and right arms (his own body is pushed forwards).
5. Then follows a right-fisted punch (cross) at A's chin.
6. D then grabs hold of A's neck from round the right hand side of A's head...
7. ...and delivers a knee kick at A's head.

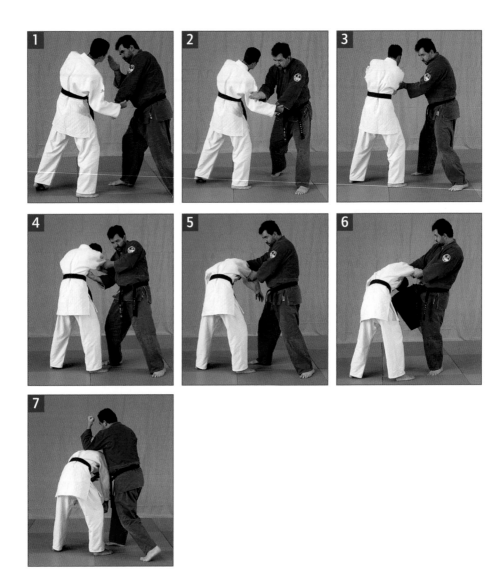

1. A executes a right uppercut at D's spleen. D counters with a left forearm block downwards and outwards, making a hand jab at the eyes at the same time.
2. With his right hand he brings it further on in to the inside...
3. ...and checks it with the left.
4. D does a right-fisted uppercut to the liver.
5. Then, the right hand grabs A's neck and pulls it downwards on to a knee kick.
6. An elbow strike downwards on the spine ends the combination.

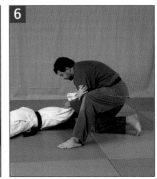

1. A executes a right-fisted punch (cross) at the head, leading with his left leg. D counters this with sweep of the left hand inwards, delivering a right-fisted punch (gunting) at the right triceps at the same time.

2.-3. Using the left arm, he brings the right arm downwards and outwards...

4. ...to execute a twisting arm lock (stretched arm lock).

5. From here D brings A straight down to the ground and immobilizes him.

1. A executes a left-fisted punch (jab), leading with his left leg. D counters with a right arm sweeping block inwards.
2. A executes a further punch with his right fist (cross).
3. D also blocks the right-fisted punch and sweeps it outwards to the right.
   D pushes the right arm upwards with his right arm.
   This is followed by a left-fisted uppercut at A's chin.
4. D executes a right-footed sweep as in this position A's right leg is unweighted.
5. A knee kick to A's ribs or head ends this combination.

7.2.4 KNEE TECHNIQUES (HIZA-GERI, HIZA-ATE)

- Atemi techniques with the lifted, bent knee.
- Execution as a straight thrust (kick) or a semi-circular (jab) movement and can be combined with strikes in all directions – vertically to horizontally.

7.2.4.1 Knee Kick

1. A grabs hold of both wrists in a forward stance.

2. D executes an escape movement with both hands simultaneously (in the direction of A's thumb)...

3. ...and then grabs hold of the opponent's wrists.

4. D pulls A's wrists towards him and at the same time delivers a right knee kick at A's upper body.

5. D lays the flat of his right hand on A's neck, and...

6. ...pulls A's head underneath his left armpit (the flat of his own right hand is held up under his armpit);

   • The left hand is slipped round from underneath around A's neck and grabs hold of his own right wrist.

   • D closes his knees together to give some protection to his genitalia...

   • ...and ends the combination with a forward headlock.

1. A executes a right shinbone kick (low kick) to the front of D's left thigh. D takes a lunge step with his right leg forwards to the right and at the same time counters to A's shinbone kick with his own left-legged shinbone kick to A's inside left thigh.
2. D grips A's left shoulder with his left arm...
3. ...and delivers a left-legged knee kick to A's upper body.
4. D executes a right arm elbow strike at A's head.
5. D places his left leg to the rear...
6. ...and ends the combination with a shinbone kick (low kick) to A's right thigh or delivers a roundhouse kick at A's head.

7.2.4.2 Jabbing with the Knee

1. A executes a left-fisted punch (jab).
   D blocks this, sweeping with his right arm inwards.
2. A executes a right-fisted punch (cross).
3. D blocks this, sweeping with his left arm inwards.

4. A's neck is gripped on the inside and pulled down with the right hand.
5. Right knee jab at A's head.
6. Kick with the right foot at A's left knee...
7. ...causing A to fall over backwards.

1. A does a frontal bear hug, pinning in D's arms.
2. D carries out a right-legged kick with his foot (stomping movement) on the bridge of A's left foot.
3. D places both hands on A's hip bones and pushes himself away downwards and rearwards...
4. ...and from this position, delivers a knee jab to A's genitalia.
5. D brings his left arm clockwise round A's right arm and does a twisting arm lock (stretched arm lock).
    • With his right hand, D presses A's head about 45° forwards and downwards in order to avoid a counter-attack against his own legs.

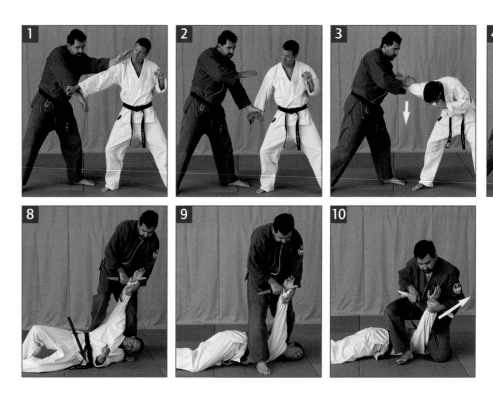

1. A executes a knife attack diagonally at hip height from left to right.
   D executes a right forearm block downwards and outwards to the right, while at the same time carrying out a hand jab at the eyes...
2. ...followed by carrying out a left hand sweeping block outwards...
3. ...leading on to applying a twisting arm lock (stretched arm lock)...
4. ...and disarming A.
5.-7. D brings A down towards the floor with a twist throw and...
8. ...climbs with his right leg over A's upper body...
9. ...and turns him onto his stomach...
10. ...ending the combination with a stretched arm lock.

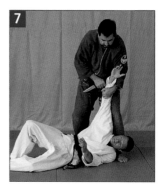

7.2.5 STOMPING KICK TECHNIQUES (MAE-FUMI-KOMI)

- Pulling the knee up and then stretching the leg and with impetus from the hips.
- The foot turned outwards hits the target with the sole.
- Forward movement by the opponent is stopped by the thrusting kick against the knee, thigh or groin or alternatively a standing opponent is put off-balance.

1. A executes the start of an attack at D's neck. D carries out a left stomping kick at A's right groin...

2. ...followed by a right-fisted punch (cross) to the head...
3. ...as well as a left-fisted punch (jab) at the stomach.
4. D places his left leg to the rear...
5. ...and ends the combination with a roundhouse foot kick to his head...
6. ...or a right-legged shinbone kick (low-kick) at A's upper body.

1. A executes a right-legged shinbone kick (low-kick) at D's left thigh. D carries out a stomping kick with his left leg at A's right groin...
2. ...followed by a right-fisted punch (cross) at the head...
3. ...followed by a double leg takedown; D kneels on his right knee in front of A having placed his left leg next to A's right leg. D grabs round both legs at the height of the hollows of the knees and pulls them together so they form an 'X'.
4. By pressing against the legs D makes A fall over backwards...
5. ...and moves into the side position and ends the combination with a bent arm lock.

1. A executes a frontal kick with the foot at D's stomach. D counters with a left forearm block downwards and inwards, while at the same time doing a step turn 90° backwards.
2. This is followed by a right-footed stomping kick at the hollow in the back of the knee.
3. The foot stays held into the hollow of the knee so that A cannot stand up. A headlock ends the combination.

7.2.6 FRONT KICK TECHNIQUES (MAE-GERI, KIN-GERI)

- After lifting the knee and stretching out the leg, the foot is brought on to the target.
- Striking surfaces can be the instep, the balls of the feet or the heel.
- Possible ways of carrying out the kick:
  In a straight line with a pronounced push forwards of the hips (front kick, Mae-geri) or in a circular motion as a snapping movement (rising kick, Kin-geri) from the joint of the knee, or a mix of both.
- Execution is carried out at least at a horizontal height or higher.

1. A executes a shinbone kick at D's left thigh.
2.-3. D pulls his left leg back just in time and sweeps the attacking leg outwards with his right leg.
4.-5. D ends the combination with a front kick at A's backside or with a rising kick in to A's genitals from behind.

1. A executes the start of an attack on the neck.
2. D knocks both arms crossed over downwards...
3. ...delivers a right-footed rising kick frontally at A's genitalia...
4. ...followed by a right-fisted punch (cross) to the head.
5. The right hand grabs A's neck round the right side of his head and pulls A's head downwards onto a right-legged knee kick.
6. Then, D places his right leg to the rear...
7.-8. ...and ends the combination with a shinbone kick (low kick) to A's front leg.

7.3   LEVERING TECHNIQUES – Locks

7.3.1   STRETCHED ARM LOCK (UdE-GATAME)

(Carried out with the opponent on the ground)

- Extension of the opponent's elbow joint by pulling the wrist and exerting pressure on the elbow joint.

- The defender applies the levered lock on the opponent as he lies on the ground.

- It is not necessary that the defender also has to be in the ground position.

- Possible ways of carrying out the lever hold: Any type of arm lock that can be chosen where the opponent is in the ground position.

- The techniques carried out when standing and when the opponent is on the ground can be identical (i.e., two x body lever hold)

7.3.1.1 Execution in the Standing Position

1. A executes a strike with a stick coming in from up to the right downwards to the head.

2.-3. Using the three step contact (Hubud), D brings the attacking arm inwards:
    - Left forearm block outwards.
    - The right hand is brought up under A's right arm.
    - Using a sweeping motion (like a windscreen wiper) with the right arm, A's right arm is brought out to the right...
    - ...and the right elbow joint is held pinned by the left hand.

4. The right hand grabs A's right wrist.

5. By pulling the wrist, the arm is stretched and pressure applied to the elbow and a stretched arm lock is put in place while standing.

6.   D brings A down on to the ground using the lock...

7.-8. ...places his right leg over A's right arm...

9.   ...and wraps the right arm round his right leg and ends the combination by applying a crossed over lock with the leg immobilizing the opponent.

1. A grabs D by both lapels.
2. D delivers a right-fisted punch (cross) at A's stomach and at the same time grabs hold of A's right wrist with his left hand.
3. D slides his left elbow over A's right arm...
4. ...also grabbing A's right wrist with his right hand...

   ...and then takes a small step to the right...

   ...creating pressure downwards onto A's elbow with his left arm and carries out a body lock (stretched arm lock).

1. A executes a strike with a stick coming in from up from the left inwards to D's head.
2. With his left hand D brings (sweeping motion) the hand with the weapon in a clockwise direction downwards and outwards to the left...
3. ...with a twisting arm lock (stretched arm lock).
4. D pulls A down to the ground in a straight line...
5. ...and disarms him with his right hand...

   ...and immobilizes the attacker on the ground with a twisting arm lock (stretched arm lock).

1. A grabs hold of D's diagonally opposed wrist.
2. D counters with a left-footed kick at the right shinbone.
3. D brings his own leg further over to the right and places it down at an angle of 90° to A. D also brings A's right arm forwards and downwards...
4. ...and, in a further movement, brings the right arm over his own left shoulder with a steady pull...
5. ...and applies a stretched arm lock over his own shoulder.
6. D, then, turns clockwise round further...

7. ...and brings A down to the ground with a 'sword' throw.
8. D pulls A's right wrist upwards and places his right hand on A's elbow.
9. By pulling on the hand and applying pressure on the elbow, he immobilizes A with this stretched arm lock.

1. A executes a knife attack coming in from up from the left inwards to D's neck.
2. D counters blocking the attack with the back of the left hand at the same time delivering a right-handed jab with the fingers at A's eyes.
3. With a sweeping motion D brings the hand with the weapon in a clockwise direction outwards to the left, and takes a step forwards to the right...
4. ...and checks A with a reverse body lock (stretched arm lock).
    D takes the knife from A with his right hand...
5. ...makes a step turn about 180° and traps A's hand using a twisting bent hand lock.
6. D places the pommel of the knife near to A's right elbow...
7. ...and brings A down on to the ground with a stretched arm lock.

7.3.1.2 Arm Lock and Execution in the Ground Position

1. A pushes D down towards the ground and applies a two-handed stranglehold. A is positioned between D's legs (guard position), who replies by clamping his legs round A in the region of the kidneys.
2. D delivers a jab with the fingers of the hand at A's head, while pinning A's right arm against his own body with his right forearm.

3. D brings A's right arm round to the left side of his body (in the direction of the groin) and immobilizes the arm with the right hand. D grabs hold of A's head with his left hand (round the neck from the right side of the head so that A cannot stand up).

4. D now rolls his left hand round A's head and pushes it to the left side.
5. D turns his body over about 90° to the right on the ground...
6. ...swings his left leg over A's head, brings his right leg very close to A's left arm i.e., the left leg is lying on A's back and the hollow of his own knee is positioned next to A's left arm. D pulls both of his feet back and pushes his heels on to the ground.
7. Now, D's left hand takes over the immobilization of A's forearm:
   • A's right arm is stretched and the left arm is pinned against D's upper body. This is because, by using the forearm, more power can be exerted this way than when the arm is held by the hand.
   • D grabs round A's left thigh with the right hand.
   • By stretching the hips, a side-stretch lever (stretched arm lock) is applied.

1. A executes a bear hug pinning D's arms down.
2. After D has delivered a stamping thrust on A's left foot in order to give him a shock...
3. ...he pushes on A's pelvis bones with both arms to get some space between himself and A.
4. After this, D delivers a knee-kick at A's genitalia.
5. D's left hand wraps itself clockwise round A's right arm and holds on round the elbow joint. D's left hand is placed on the right hand and a stretched arm lock (standing) is applied.
6.-7. D swings his left leg over A's head and he executes a sling throw.
8. He then conducts a right-footed stamp on A's lower ribcage...
9. ...places his foot forwards over A and turns him onto his stomach...
10. ...ending the combination with an arm lock over the groin.

1. A pushes D in the direction of the ground and delivers a right-fisted punch at D's head. A is positioned between D's legs. D has A under control by applying a scissors-leg clinch round the area of the kidneys.
2. By pulling up on his legs, D brings A forwards off-balance and sweeps the attacking arm to the right with the left hand.
3. D is holding A's right arm and pushes his left foot under A's head.
4. By pushing the hips forward and clamping the arm between the legs while lifting the arms towards the ceiling (with the little finger pointing upwards) a twisting lever (stretched arm lock) is applied.

1. A executes a frontal headlock from a side position.
2. D gouges into A's right eye with his left thumb. A lets go of his grip and stands upright.
3. D executes a backwards roll so that A falls backward.
4. D moves straight away into the scarf hold (Kesa-gatame)...
5. ...presses his left hand onto the ground close to A's neck...
6. ...stretches his upper body upwards (thus freeing the grip), swings his left leg over A's head...
7. ...and applies a side-stretch lock (stretched arm lock).

1. A applies a frontal headlock on D.
2. D delivers a hand jab at A's neck and frees himself from the headlock with the left arm, and pulls his head away...
3. ...grabbing between A's legs with his right arm holding on to his bottom/lower back. The left hand is placed diagonally over the right neck side on to A's back.
4. D lifts A up by stretching up from his knees...
   ...turns him in to the horizontal position...
5. ...and lets him drop...
6. ...and goes down on top of him in the straddle position...

7. ...sliding the right knee up over A's left upper arm...

8. ...placing his left foot next to A's ear (the heel is pointing at the neck), and applies a stretched arm lock over the groin to immobilize the opponent.

7.3.2 Bent Arm Lock (Ude-garami)

- Any extension applied on the opponent's bent arm having an effect on the elbow and/or the shoulder joint.

- The immobilizing technique must be made so that the opponent is pinned in his position at that moment and has an extremely limited ability to counter-attack.

7.3.2.1 Execution in the Standing Position

1. A executes a right-fisted punch with the back of the hand at D's head.
2. D grabs A's right wrist with his right hand, brings his left arm round A's right arm, and grabs his own right wrist so that a bent arm lock is applied.
3. D pulls A sharply forward to bring him off-balance...
4. ...and using the impetus of A's movement, he pulls back his own arm and brings it in the direction of A's right shoulder. As he does this he delivers a right elbow strike to A's head...
5. ...then brings A down to the ground with a bent arm lock.
6. D kneels on A with both knees and immobilizes him with a bent hand lock.

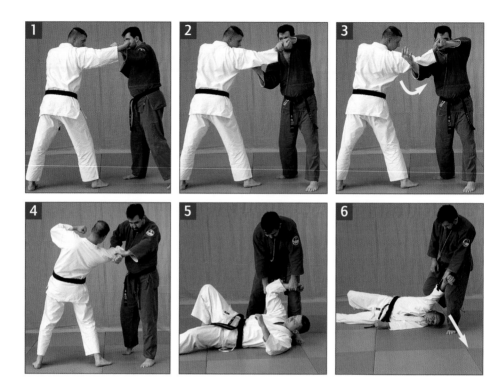

1. A executes a right hook punch at D's head. D counters with a left forearm block outwards...

2. ...grabs hold of A's right wrist with his left hand and delivers a right-handed knuckle punch (gunting) at A's triceps.

3. D places the middle finger of the right hand in the crease of the elbow from the outside...

4. ...and presses with his left hand against the arm, pulling the elbow upwards with his right one so that a bent arm lock can be applied.

5. Using this arm lock, D brings A down to the ground...

6. ...places his right shinbone on the right upper arm...

7. ...and turns A over on to his stomach. D immobilizes A on the ground with a stretched arm lock.

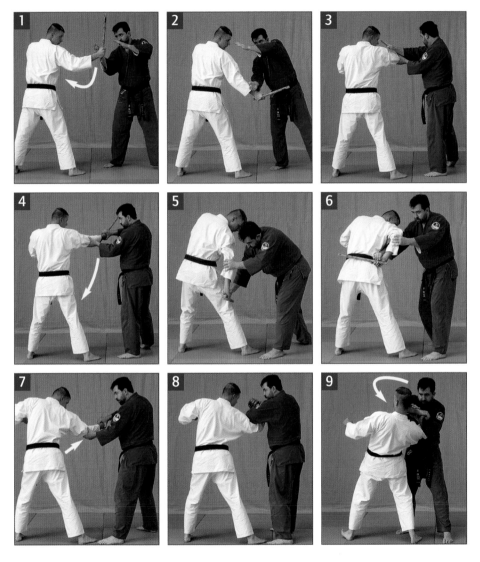

1. A executes an attack at the head with a stick coming down in at the outside of D's head.
2. D counters with a right backhand sweep counterclockwise downwards and outwards, while at the same time delivering a left-handed jab at the eyes.
3. D places the left hand underneath the right elbow and delivers a right-handed jab at the eyes.
4. He grabs A's arm holding the weapon with his right hand.
5. He brings the arm in the direction of A's body and delivers a strike with the stick at A's shinbone/knee.

6. The arm is brought further behind A...
   ...and the stick is placed on A's back in the region of the kidneys...
7. ...while A's right hand is pulled closely along his upper body, thus being able to disarm A (over his body).
8. D reaches over A's right arm with his left hand...
   ...and grabs hold of his own right wrist...
   ...and applies a bent arm lock.
9. The arm is brought up towards A's right shoulder, while at the same time delivering a right elbow strike at A's head.
10. After this, A is brought down to the ground with a bent arm lock...
11. ...and immobilized on the ground with a bent hand lock.

1. A executes a knife attack at D's stomach.
2. D counters with a right forearm block downwards and outwards with the hand open and the forearm tensed. At the same time he delivers a finger jab at A's eyes (disrupting action).
3. D grabs hold of the ball of the right thumb with his left hand...

4. ...brings the hand holding the weapon counterclockwise upwards and outwards to the left...

5. ...takes the knife out of A's hand with his right hand...

6. ...brings his right arm counterclockwise round A's arm and places the pommel of the knife against A's chest.

7. D gets round behind A's back, grabs round A's neck deep into his lapel.

8. With a stomping kick D forces A to go into a kneeling position, keeping his right foot in the hollow of A's knee so that he cannot stand up.

1.   A is standing behind D and is threatening him with a pistol placed into D's back. D puts his hands up...
2.   ...turns round clockwise to the right...
3.   ...and brings the right arm counterclockwise upwards round A's arm holding the weapon, and applies a bent arm lock...
4.-5. ...disarming A with his left hand...
6.   ...and concludes the technique by striking A's head with the pistol grip.

7.3.2.2 Bent Arm Lock and Execution as an Immobilization Technique

1. A executes an attack at D's legs with both hands.
2. D stops A by placing his left hand on A's head and bringing his right hand underneath A's arm onto his back...
3. ...and lays his right hand on his left hand (the one on the back of A's head), and causes A to fall by applying pressure forwards and downwards.
4. D moves to the right-hand side of A's head...
5. ...then kneels down with his right knee on A's upper arm, brings the left hand to A's left wrist. D now puts his left knee over to the other side of A's head (A's head is clamped between D's legs), and pushes the right hand through underneath A's left hand and grabs hold of his own left wrist (bent arm lock).
   D pulls A's left hand in the direction of his right shoulder so that the bent arm lock is effective as an immobilization technique.

1. A gives D a clip around the ear with the right hand.
2. D counters with a diagonal right hand sweep to the left and outside.
3. The left hand takes over checking the right arm.
4. D carries out a strike with the edge of the right hand at the neck.
5. D executes a reaping leg sweep...
6.-7. ...with his right leg around the left leg and kneels down.
8. He then moves into a straddle position (side-mount, cross-position). His own left leg is crossed outwards over the right leg

9. The right leg is then pulled under the left leg.
10. A's right wrist is then grabbed hold of by the right hand.

   The left is thrust through under A's right arm and gets hold of his own right wrist. His own wrist is pressed upwards (like revving up on a motor bike). A's right elbow is pulled down to his right hip. The right hand is pinned to the ground, and A's right upper arm is pressed upwards by the left hand and a bent arm lock is applied to effect immobilization.

1. A takes D's hand and tries to crush it.
2. D gives A a surprise shock by kicking A's right shinbone with his right foot...
3. ...and then places his right foot forwards behind A...

   ...twists A's hand that was crushing his counterclockwise...
4.-5. ...and brings A down to the ground with reverse tilting hand lock.
6. D then follows up by making a kick at A's head sideways.

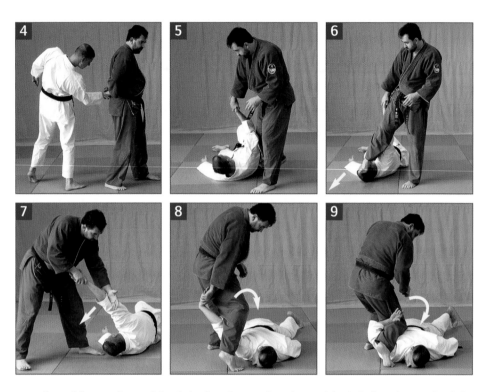

7. After this, D places his right leg forwards, places his left hand on A's right elbow...

8. ...and turns him over on to his stomach.
   D places his right leg over A's outstretched arm...

9. ...and wraps the arm round the right leg...
   ...kneels down and applies a crossover grip
   (bent arm lock) with the leg.

1. A has brought D down and is positioned between his legs.
   A is supported by placing the hand of his right arm down on the ground.
2.-3. D grabs hold of the right wrist with his left hand, brings A's left hand outwards to the right...
4. ...and lifts his upper body up towards the left, grasping over A's right arm with his right arm...
5. ...and takes hold of his own left wrist...
6. ...bringing the hips outwards a little to the left, and turns the bent arm (bent arm lock) in the direction of A's left shoulder and clamps A with his legs round his back.

1. A executes a right-fisted hook punch at D's head.
2. D counters carrying out a left-arm passive block...
3. ...makes a right-footed lunging step forwards, grabs over A's left arm with his right arm. For this, D is standing at an angle of 90° to A. D's head is pressing against A's chest and his left hand is holding A's right hand.
4. Now D moves his hips round in front of A. D remains leaning forwards as he does this.
5.-7. D throws A down to the ground using a hip throw...

8. ...and adopts the straddle position, hooking his legs under A's...
9.-10. ...and presses A's right arm onto the ground using both of his arms.
11. The left arm is pushed through under A's right arm and D grabs hold of his own right wrist, applying a bent arm lock. D levers his own wrist upwards (as if he were revving up on a motor bike), pulls A's elbow in the direction of the right hip, and immobilizes A on the ground with a bent arm lock.

7.3.2.3 Bent Arm Lock and Execution as a Technique Able to Move the Opponent About ('Transporting Lever')

1. A executes a strike with a stick coming horizontally inwards from outside right at D's hips.
2. D sweeps the arm holding the weapon diagonally downwards and outwards with his right arm simultaneously delivering a finger jab at the eyes (disrupting action).
3. The left hand takes over the job of holding the right wrist (checking the arm holding the weapon)...

4. ...and the right hand levers the stick with a forearm motion out of A's right hand.
5. In the same movement, a right-handed finger jab at the eyes is delivered.
6. D brings his right arm in a circular motion outwards, downwards and then inwards, and grips into the crease of A's right elbow with the middle finger of the right hand...

7. ...and forces A down on the ground with a bent arm lock. D places his right hand on A's right elbow...
8. ...and turns him over on to his stomach.
9. D places the left near to the right elbow, holding on to the left shoulder with his right hand as he does this so that A cannot turn himself round...
10. ...and by lifting with his own left arm makes A stand up, while changing over to holding A's head with his right hand and pulls it into the neck. With a crossed over grip (bent arm lock as a 'transporting lever') he moves A along.

1. A grabs hold of D's left lapel with his right hand and delivers a left-fisted punch (in-swinging hook) at D's head.
2. D counters by doing a right forearm block outwards to the right. At the same time, the left hand pins A's right hand to his own upper body.
3. D delivers a punch at the solar plexus.
4. D's right hand grabs hold of A's upper arm from behind...
5. ...and pulls this forward, pushing the forearm backwards to the rear at the same time.
6. D grabs hold of A's right upper arm with his left hand near to the elbow...
7. ...and ends the combination with a crossed over grip (bent arm lock 'transporting lever').

1. A applies a forearm stranglehold on D's neck from behind.
2. D delivers a jab with his left thumb at A's left eye.
3. D frees himself from the stranglehold...
4. ...and moves from under A's arm to the rear...
5. ...bringing and twisting A's right arm up behind his back in a bent arm lock, grasps with his left hand into A's eyes from above, and moves A along with the bent arm lock in combination with pressure on the eyes (gouging the nerve point).

7.3.3   Major Outer Hold (O-Soto-osae)

- Leverage achieved by extension of the neck and the lumbar vertebra.

- One hand applies pressure on the front of the head while the other hand creates counter pressure in the region of the lumbar vertebra.

- For the execution of these techniques, the defender is standing sideways on to the attacker.

1. A grabs hold of D from behind with his right hand on D's collar.

2. D takes a step turn backwards while at the same time delivering a backhanded blow to the nose with the left hand. This makes A lose his balance backwards.
3. D is standing at a 90° angle to A. The left hand is placed into the lumbar area while a palm heel blow is delivered to the chin with the right hand.
4. By bending the body over further in a major outer hold D forces A down to the ground.
5. An inside stretched arm lock (coiling arm) ends the combination.

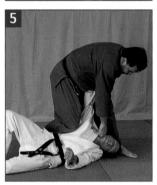

1. Leading with his left foot, A executes a left-fisted punch, which D sweeps away to the inside with his right hand.
2. A delivers a second left-fisted punch. D punches up under A's punch arm with a left-handed upwards palm heel hook at A's chin, covering his own head simultaneously with his right hand.
3. D delivers a palm heel punch at A's head with his right hand and at the same time places his left hand onto A's lumbar vertebra...
4. ...forcing A to bend over backwards onto the ground.
5. D applies a knuckle press as a concluding technique.

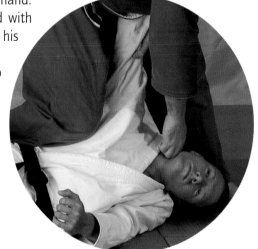

7.4 Throwing Techniques

7.4.1 Major Outer Throw (O-Soto-otoshi)

- The balance is broken either backwards, sideways, by pulling or by pushing (pressure) or by using an Atemi technique.
- The defender, who is standing sideways next to the attacker, places the leg nearest to his opponent between his legs and pushes him down to the ground.
- Free choice of the type of grip to be used.

1. A grabs hold of D's hand opposite him.
2. D carries out a freeing action from the grip with his left hand, while at the same time taking a lunge step to the left and delivering a right-handed strike with the edge of the hand at the left carotid artery.

3. D places his right leg behind A's right leg...
4. ...and forces A down to the ground using this leg trip.
5. D places his right hand on A's elbow...

6. ...and brings him over on to his stomach by pulling the hand and applying pressure on the elbow.
7. D kneels down on the left side of A's head with his right knee pressing on the area between A's shoulders and immobilizes him with a twisting bent hand lock.

1. A executes a right-footed low-kick at D's thigh. D pulls the heel of his left foot close up to his bottom and then straightens the knee in the direction of the attacking leg.
2. D delivers a right-fisted punch at A's chin.
3. The right hand grabs hold of A's neck and the left hand grabs the upper arm just underneath the triceps. The right leg is placed behind A's right leg...
4. ...and forces A down to the ground using this leg trip.
5. D climbs over A with both legs (first, the left one and then the right one over the neck/upper body) and immobilizes A with a sideways lock (stretched arm lock). It is important that the knees are pressed together, the hips are raised and that A's little finger is pulled downwards.

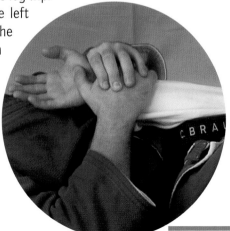

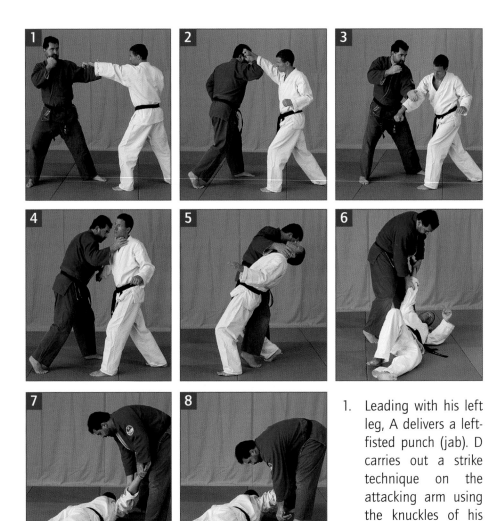

1. Leading with his left leg, A delivers a left-fisted punch (jab). D carries out a strike technique on the attacking arm using the knuckles of his left fist (gunting). The strike is brought in a semi-circular motion and delivered at the forearm so that probability of hitting the target is increased.

2. A now delivers a right-fisted punch (cross) and D blocks it passively coming up with his right arm (salute-block).

3. The left hand grabs A's right upper arm...

4. ...while the right hand grabs hold of A's neck/head.

5. The right leg is placed behind A's right leg...

...and he forces A down to the ground using this leg trip.

6. D places his right hand on A's elbow and the left hand grabs the wrist...

7. ...and by pulling the hand and applying pressure on the elbow A is brought over on to his stomach.

8.-10. Using a wrist lock as a 'transport lever'...

11. ...in combination with pressure on the nerves underneath the ear, A can be moved about.

7.4.2 Major Hip Throw (O-goshi) or Loin Wheel (Koshi-guruma)

- The balance is broken forwards by pulling or by using an Atemi technique.
- Perform a twisting movement from the parallel stance to avoid getting the center of gravity of the body in the wrong place.
- The throw is carried out by stretching the legs and scooping up the opponent and turning the upper body.
- Stance when executing the hip throw: Directly in front of the opponent with the throw flowing over the hips.
- Stance when executing the loin wheel: Sideways to the opponent to one side with the throw flowing over one's back.
- Free choice of the type of grip to be used.

7.4.2.1 Loin Wheel

1. A grabs D's lapel with his right hand and delivers a left-fisted punch (cross).
2. D grabs hold of A's right hand with his left hand and sweeps away the punching hand with his right hand inwards.
3. Changeover to holding A's left arm with the left hand and bring/pull it downwards (the attacker's arms are now crossed over).
4. The punching hand is grabbed again by the right hand. The body is now turned inwards...

5.-8. ...and a loin wheel is applied.

9. D climbs over A with both legs (first the left and then the right)...
10. ...and the combination is concluded with a sideways lock (stretched arm lock).

1. A is carrying out a stranglehold with both hands from behind.
2. D lifts the left hand up vertically and pins A's left hand against his own neck.
3. Now, D turns counterclockwise in front of A. The turn serves to free the grip.
4. D reaches over A's arms with his left arm.
5. The right arm is brought round A's neck. D turns to carry out the loin wheel so that the hips are pushed outwards...
6.-7. ...and throws A forwards.

8. D adopts the straddle/mount position...
9. ...hooks both legs under A's, places the right arm under A's neck, places the right hand on his own left biceps, places the left hand on the right-hand side of A's face with his own right-hand side of his face on his left hand. D's shoulders are pushed up under/in front of A's jawbone. D now applies pressure forwards so that the neck lock becomes effective.

7.4.2.2 Hip Throw

1. A is carrying out a stranglehold with both hands from the side.
2. D counters with an elbow strike sideways to the right.
3. D pulls A against him and turns into a parallel stance.

4.-5. D throws A to the ground with a hip throw.

6.-7. D carries out a kick against the lower ribcage and turns A onto his stomach...

8. ...and ends the combination with a stretched arm lock over the groin.

1. A delivers a right hook punch. D counters with a left forearm block outwards.
2. This is followed by a right-legged lunging step forwards to the right so that D is standing at 90° to A. D has his right arm over A's left arm and his head on A's chest with his left hand holding A's right hand.
3. D now brings his hips forward. The upper body leaning forward as he does this...
4.-6. ...and he executes a hip throw.

7.	D grabs A's right wrist with his left hand and with his right hand he presses against A's right elbow.

8.	By pulling on the wrist and pressing on the elbow, A is turned over onto his stomach.

9.	D places his left hand close to the right elbow and applies a crossed over lock (bent arm lock) on the ground.

10.	The right hand is holding A's left shoulder so that he cannot turn it to the rear to deliver an elbow strike.

11.-12. From this position, D pushes forwards and makes A stand up. With the crossover grip, A can be now moved about ('transport lever').

7.4.3 MAJOR OUTER REAPING THROW (O-SOTO-GARI)

- The balance is broken backwards, sideways, by pulling and pushing (pressure) or by using an Atemi technique.
- The defender, standing to one side of the attacker, swings the leg nearest to the opponent from outside, through between the attackers legs and sweeps the standing leg away forcing him to fall down sideways to the rear.
- Free choice of the type of grip to be used.

1. A grabs hold of D's wrist opposite him with his left hand and with his right fist he clips D's ear. D counters with a left forearm block upwards and outwards.
2. This is followed by getting out of the grip as he rolls his own right elbow over A's arm.

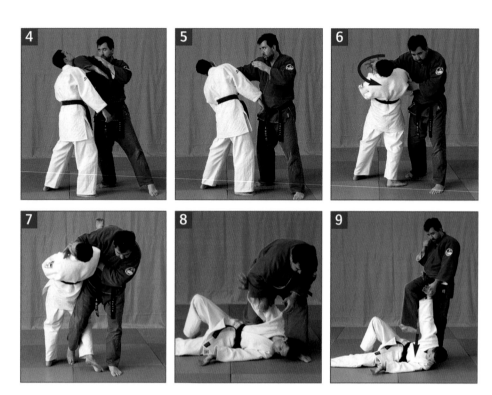

3. After this, D delivers a right elbow strike to the chest and at the same time a left-handed jab at the neck.
4. D bends the elbow upwards to A's chin.
5. Using his right hand, D turns A's face to the right. As he does this, D turns himself to the left and takes hold of A's free, right arm.
6. A's center of gravity has now been put off-balance 45° to the rear...
7.-8. ...and a major outer reaping throw is carried out.
9. As a concluding technique, a downwards kick is executed.

1. A delivers a right hook punch. D counters this with a left forearm block outwards...

2. ...while at the same time delivering a right-fisted palm heel punch at A's head.

3. D reaches over the punching arm with his left hand and grabs hold of the triceps, pulling A left and backwards off-balance.

4.-6. D uses a major outer reaping and throws him sideways and backwards onto the ground...

7. ...kneels down with his left knee on A's neck and the right knee on A's right side and immobilizes A with an inner arm lock (stretched arm lock).

1. A grabs hold of both of D's lapels.
2. D delivers a right-fisted punch at the solar plexus.
3. D pushes the right hand between A's arms and grabs hold of his own right hand with his left hand from the outside...
4. ...and executes a grip break with a hefty movement of the body first of all to the left...

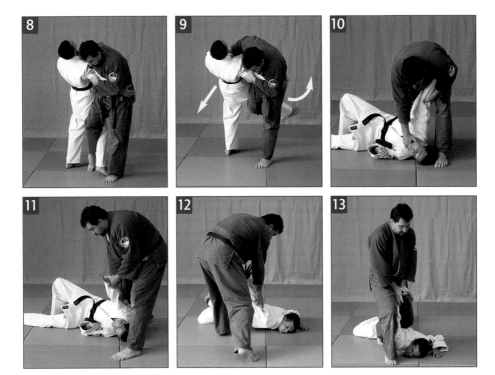

5.　　...and then to the right...

6.　　...grabbing A's right upper arm in the region of the triceps with his left hand, and with his right hand A's left lapel or his neck and brings A off-balance 45° round to the left and rear...

7.-10.　...and uses a major outer reaping throw to bring him down to the ground sideways and backwards.

11.-12.　D turns A over on to his stomach by gripping hold of the right wrist and applying pressure on A's right elbow with his right hand...

13.　　...and immobilizes him with a twisted bent wrist lock.

8 Reaction/Counter-Reaction Technique

8.1 Changeover from the Bent Arm Lock (Ude-garami) to the Stretched Arm Lock (Ude-gatame)

- Demonstration with a partner. Starting position: Opposite hand is brought from the outside to grab the partner's wrist. Pressure is applied on the elbow joint using the free hand, the edge of the hand or forearm.
- When the arm that is to be locked is bent in the direction of the upper body, the student reacts changing over to a bent arm lock (locking grip).
- When the arm is stretched out again, then there is a changeover to a stretched arm lock again.
- The demonstration is done by both arms.

9 PURSUING TECHNIQUES (GAESHI-WAZA)

9.1 Avoiding Being Thrown Forwards

9.1.2 By Dodging

- The student starts for example a hip throw on his partner.
- By dodging sideways away from the partner, during or after the turning in phase, the lift and the throw is avoided.
- The student must be able to demonstrate both possibilities of dodging – both to the left and the right.
- Follow up techniques by the exercising student can be done, but are not essential.

AGAINST THE direction of THE THROW

IN THE direction of THE THROW

9.1.3 By Blocking

- The student starts for example a loin wheel on his partner:
  a) By dropping the hips down and pushing forwards during the turning in phase.
  b) By applying counter pressure (e.g., Atemi) using the ball of the hands against the hips.
  c) By dropping the hips down and pushing them forward at the same time during the turn in phase and using the balls of the hands against the hips so that a complete turn in for the throw cannot be made.
- The student must be able to demonstrate the two possibilities.

By dropping the hips down

In the direction of the throw

10   FREE SELF-DEFENSE

10.1   FREE SELF-DEFENSE AGAINST HOLDING GRIPS (DUO SERIES 1)

- The defender may defend himself in any way he is capable of.
- The choice of which defense technique is to be used, is up to the student.
- The attacks should be done as dynamically as possible; defense should be done as an immediate reaction to an attack.
- Points to watch for: Effectiveness, dynamics, correct reach used and general impression.

10.1.1 ATTACK 1: ONE OF THE WRISTS   IS GRIPPED BY BOTH HANDS

1.-2. D executes a left-handed jab at the neck, freeing the grip with his right hand.
3. The left hand hits the opponent's arm away and a right-handed palm heel punch is delivered to the chin.
4. D places his right leg behind A's right leg...

5.-6. ...and he forces A down to the ground using this trip technique.

7. D climbs over A with both legs (first, left then right leg)...

8. ...and immobilizes A using a sideways stretch lock (stretched arm lock) on the ground.

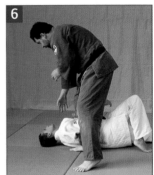

1.-3. D brings A round in a clockwise direction with his left hand placed on A's neck.
4. D suddenly turns back into the original position...
5. ...brings his right arm in the direction of A's neck and places his left arm on A's lumbar vertebra area...
6. ...forcing A to fall backwards by pushing his body over.

1.-2. D's left hand reaches through A's hands and grabs hold of his own right hand...

3. ...and then he rips the hand upwards (breaking the grip).

4. D executes a right back-of-the-hand punch at A's head.

5. Then D blocks both of A's arms with his right arm...

6. ...delivering a left-fisted punch at A's head.

10.1.2 ATTACK 2: Single Handed Lapel Grip (diagonal)

1.-2. D delivers a right-handed clip on the ear and brings the hand over further to the left side, while at the same time grabbing hold of A's right wrist with his left hand.

3. D brings his right arm over the right arm (in the region of the elbow) and applies a bent arm lock.

4. The left hand breaks the grip on the right wrist and pushes the right side of A's face to the left.

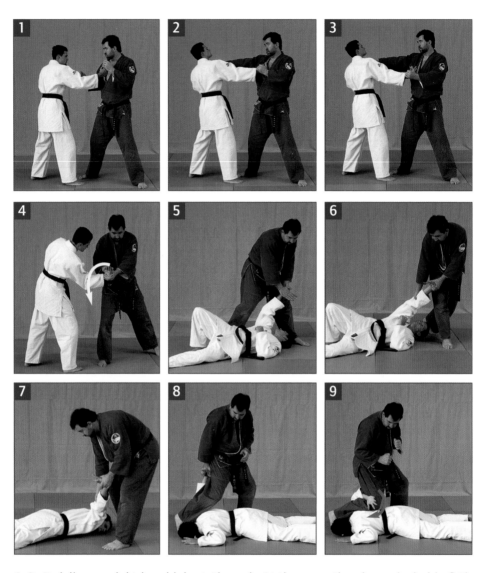

1.-2. D delivers a right hand jab at A's neck. At the same time he grabs hold of A's right wrist with his left hand...

3. ...and frees it from his lapel.

4. D applies a bent hand lever in combination with a 90° step turn...

5.-7. ...bringing A onto his stomach by placing his left hand on A's right wrist and the right hand on his elbow.

8. D brings A's right arm round his right leg...

9. ...and immobilizes him with a crossed over grip (bent arm lock) over the leg.

1.-2. D executes a right-hand jab at the chin, and grabs hold of A's right wrist with his left hand.

3.-5. He then grabs hold of A's right hand with his right hand, and applies a twisted bent hand lock.

6. With a straight-line pull, D forces A down to the ground, and immobilizes him there with a stretched arm lock.

10.1.3 Attack 3: Frontal Strangle Using Both Hands

1.-2. D delivers a right-handed jab at the hollow of A's larynx.
3.   D then brings his right arm over A's right arm and applies a bent arm lock. He pushes A's head to the left side with his left hand.
4.   D gets round to the rear of A and grabs his left lapel with his right hand and with his left hand he grabs deep into the collar thus conducting a strangle hold using the clothing.
5.   After this, D delivers a right-legged kick into the hollow at the rear of A's right knee. Until A gives in, D leaves his right foot in the hollow of the knee to stop him standing up.

  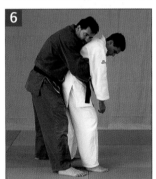

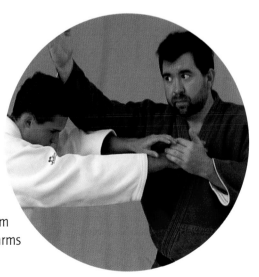

1.-2. D delivers a right-fisted punch at A's stomach.

3.-5. With his right arm coming in from outside to the inside, he strikes the arms away (circular motion).

6. D gets round to the rear of A...

7. ...lifts him up about 20 cm...

8. ...and lets him drop into his knees...

9.   ...and follows him down on to the ground, bringing both of his legs over A's and grabbing A's left arm with his left hand and bringing his right arm round in front of A's neck with his right hand placed on A's left shoulder.

10.   D pushes his left hand behind A's head (the back of the hand is behind the head) and applies a forearm stranglehold on A.

10.1.4 Attack 4: Stranglehold from the Side with Both Hands

1.-2. D delivers a right-handed jab at the hollow of A's larynx and grabs hold of the right hand with his left hand at the same time.

2.-3. Now, D rips A's right hand downwards and applies a bent hand lock.

4. The right hand grabs hold of A's right wrist and with his left hand he takes hold of his right elbow.

5.-6. D bends up A's right arm and twists him down on to his stomach. D twists A's right arm on to his back with a bent arm lock and kneels with both knees onto A's back. D could also pull A's head back with his hair.

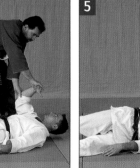

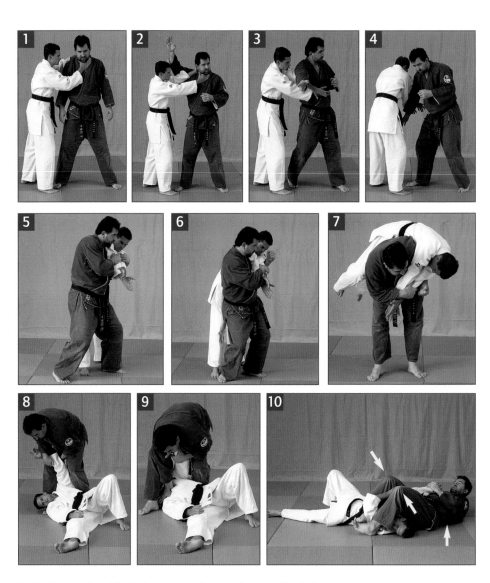

1.-2. D stretches his right arm up forwards past A's right arm.

3.   D turns abruptly to the left, breaking A's grip as he does.

4.-6. D turns on round further and pins, from underneath, both of A's arms with his left arm...

7.-8. ...and then D executes a shoulder throw...

9.   ...climbs over A's upper body with both legs (first left and then the right leg)...

10.   ...and immobilizes him with sideways stretch lock (stretched arm lock).

1.-2. D gouges into A's left eye with his right thumb (more a wiping motion)...

3. ...and sweeps A's right hand a little to the outside with his left arm...

4. ...grabs over the elbow with his right arm and sweeps both of A's arms outwards.

D then hooks his left arm upwards...

5. ...and delivers a right-fisted punch.

6. D places his left foot backwards...

7. ...and ends the combination with a right shinbone kick at A's forward leg.

10.1.5 Attack 5: A Single-handed Grab at the Jacket (in the Area of the Shoulder) from the Side

1. D brings the right arm upwards and inwards until the little finger of the opponent's hand is pointing upwards.
2. D now grabs A's left hand and applies a twist on the side of the hand.
3. D places the fingers of the right hand on A's left elbow...
   ...pulls the elbow outwards and applies a twisting hand lock.
4. This forces A down on to his knees with the combination ending by D delivering a knee kick at the attacker's chin.

1.-2. D executes a 90° step turn forwards and at the same time delivers a left-handed finger jab at the hollow of A's larynx.

3. Now D knocks A's left arm away with his left arm, and at the same time carries out a palm heel punch at A's face.

4. The left hand is laid over A's face...

5. ...and pushes his head back, while carrying out a right elbow strike at the muscles on the left of A's neck/throat.

1.-2. D executes a 90° step turn forwards and at the same time brings the fingers of his right hand in a circular outwards motion over A's eyes.

3. D brings his right arm round A's left arm...

4. ...and applies a bent arm lock.

5. D places the middle finger of his left hand in the hollow under A's left ear and applies pressure on the nerve.

11   FREE Applications

11.1   Using (hands only) Atemi Techniques

- Fighting in a standing position using exclusively the open hands (palms).
- The target area is the whole body (including the legs).
- Aim to make light contact without hard contact.
- Exercise aim: Free application of defense techniques and forms of movement.
- Protective equipment: Male students must wear lower protectors (mandatory).
- Length of Training: 1-2 minutes with partners changing over once.

11.2   Using Groundwork Techniques

- Fighting with body contact in groundwork.
- One of the partners brings the other off balance (e.g., a leg trip) onto the ground and follows him down, where fighting commences; after breaks or when changing over roles, the same starting position is used, however, each student should have the opportunity to bring his partner down once and also play the role of himself being brought down using appropriate techniques.
- Exercise aim: Free application of at least the holding and freeing techniques learned.
- The application of locking techniques (e.g., the stretched arm lock) is particularly desirable.
- The use of Atemi and techniques where pressure is applied to nerve points as well as the lifting neck lock is not allowed.
- Protective equipment: Male students must wear lower protectors (mandatory).
- Length of Training: 1-2 minutes with partners changing over once.

Literature

On my Internet web pages under www.open-mind-combat.com a list of books can be found. Those interested can gain an overview of the Martial Arts literature. The publishers of this book, Meyer & Meyer, have a large coverage of publications on the Martial Arts – see their Internet web page under www.m-m-sports.com.

Photo & Illustration Credits

Cover design: Jens Vogelsang, Aachen
Photos: Christian Braun

Christian Braun, born 1965

Profession: Systems Analyst/IT Instructor

Training Address:
Fight Academy Christian Braun
Westendstraße 15
67059 Ludwigshafen
Tel.: 0049 177 2843080

Address:
Peter-Paul-Rubens-Str. 1
67227 Frankenthal
E-Mail: Christian.Braun@open-mind-combat.com
Home: www.open-mind-combat.com

Requests for information regarding courses, private training as well as books, training knives, sticks, protective glasses and martial arts accessories should be sent to the above address.

Qualifications:
*   Head Instructor Open Mind Combat (OMC)
*   5th Dan Ju-Jutsu, Licensed JJ-Instructor, Trainer 'B' License
*   Phase 6 and Madunong Guro in the IKAEF under Jeff Espinous and Johan Skalberg
*   Instructor in Progressive Fighting Systems (Jeet Kune Do Concepts) under Paul Vunak
*   Head Coach International Luta-Livre Union for Germany
*   Luta-Livre Coach under Rolando Carrizo Ortiz
*   1st Dan Jiu-Jitsu (German Jiu-Jitsu Association)
*   Phase 2 Jun Fan Gung Fu under Ralf Beckmann
*   7th Dan Ju-Jitsu (All Japan Ju-Jitsu International Federation), Shihan, Technical Director of Combat Ju-Jitsu

Personal Security:
*   Trainer for personal security for the managing board of a big IT-Company and chemical industry in Baden-Württemberg, Germany.

Offices held:
*   1990-1991 – Trainer and Press Representative for the Ju-Jutsu Section of the Judo Association for the German State of the Pfalz (Rhineland Palatinate)
*   1999-2003 – Speaker for the Ju-Jutsu Association (Ju-Jutsu Verband Baden e.V.) in matters for Sport for Seniors and the Disabled
*   1992-today – Head of Section in the Turn- und Gefechtclub 1861 e.V. (German Gymnastics and Fencing Club 1861)

Organization:
*   Speaker on the German National Seminar of the DJJV e.V. (German Ju-Jutsu Association) 2003 and 2004
*   Speaker at German National Courses held by the DJJV e.V.
*   Speaker in the faculty of JJ Instructors Division of the DJJV e.V.
*   Member of the Trainer Team of the Ju-Jutsu Verband Baden e.V.
*   Member of the Trainer Team of the DJJV e.V. in the faculty for Sport for the Disabled

Competition Achievements in the Upper Open Weight Classes:
Between 1988-1991 several place results achieved in the Pfalz Individual Championships with 1st Place taken in 1991. Placed in Third Place, three times in the German South-West Individual Championships. 2004, placed in Fourth Place in the Lock and Choke Tournament of the European Luta-Livre-Organization in the Upper Open Weight Class. In January 2005 in Karlsruhe, placed in Second Place in the Submissao Grappling Challenge. In February 2005 in Cologne, placed in SecondPlace in the Luta-Livre German Individual Championships in the Weight Class +99 kg (Advanced Class).

www.m-m-sports.com

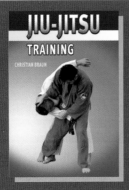

Christian Braun
Jiu-Jitsu
Training

264 pages, full-color print
1431 photos and illustrations
Paperback, 6½" x 9¼"
ISBN: 978-1-84126-179-9
$ 19.95 US
£ 14.95 UK/€ 18.95

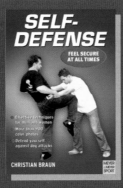

Christian Braun
Self-Defense

256 pages, full color print
935 color photos and illustrations
Paperback, 6½" x 9¼"
ISBN: 978-1-84126-246-8
$ 19.95 US
£ 14.95 UK/€ 19.95

Christian Braun
Self-Defense against
Knife Attacks

288 pages, full-color print
1700 photos and illustrations
Paperback, 6½" x 9¼"
ISBN: 978-1-84126-198-0
$ 19.95 US
£ 14.95 UK/€ 18.95